WHAT'S THE ISSUE?

FUTURE HUMANS

TOM JACKSON • CRISTINA GUITIAN

QED

Quarto is the authority on a wide range of topics.

Quarto educates, entertains and enriches the lives of our readers—enthusiasts and lovers of hands-on living.

www.quartoknows.com

Author: Tom Jackson
Illustrator: Cristina Guitian
Designers: Tracy Killick and Mike Henson
Editors: Claire Watts and Ellie Brough
Editorial Director: Laura Knowles
Creative Director: Malena Stojic
Publisher: Maxime Boucknooghe

First published in 2019 by QED Publishing,
an imprint of The Quarto Group.
The Old Brewery, 6 Blundell Street,
London, N7 9BH, United Kingdom.
T +44 (0)20 7700 6700
F +44 (0)20 7700 8066
www.QuartoKnows.com

A catalogue record for this book is available from the British Library.

ISBN 978 0 7112 4454 2

Manufactured in Guangdong, China CC082019
9 8 7 6 5 4 3 2 1

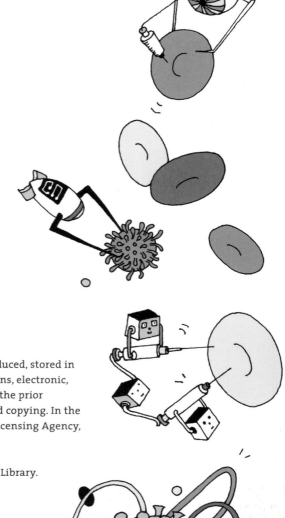

MIX
Paper from responsible sources
FSC
www.fsc.org   FSC® C008047

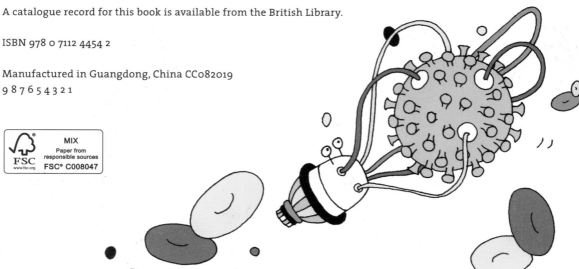

CONTENTS

AUTHOR'S NOTE

WHAT'S THE ISSUE WITH THE HUMAN BODY?

How will it change in the future? And could we one day live forever? Mortality is a complicated subject, but never fear because you are in the right place to learn more. I can't give you any simple answers, I'm afraid, but this book will help you decide for yourself what the future might hold for the human race. All I can do is tell you what I know and set out what's what and who's who.

THEN IT'S UP TO YOU TO MAKE AN INFORMED OPINION.

How we control and change our bodies – and our minds – in the future could transform the way we treat disease and disability. It could change the way we perceive the world and might even cheat death. It sounds like something you need to know about. In this book I'll break it down for you, but even then the wrongs and rights are not always clear. Every now and then, you'll get a chance to question what you've read and think about it.

WHAT DO YOU THINK?
WHAT DO YOUR FRIENDS THINK?
WHAT DO YOUR PARENTS THINK?
WHAT DOES YOUR TEACHER THINK?

Everyone and anyone can have an opinion, but not everyone's opinion will be informed. With this book, you will have the knowledge to back up your arguments.

OPINIONS MATTER, SO WHAT WILL YOURS BE?

Welcome to the future. Since you were born you've been a time traveller. A lot has changed since you began your adventure; that process of change is what the future is all about. This book looks at how technology will give us greater control over our bodies, allowing us to change them, replace parts or even do without them at all. What do you think will happen in the future? There's only one way to find out. Off we go!

WHAT'S WHAT?

WHAT'S A FUTUROLOGIST?

A person who makes a serious attempt to predict the future is called a futurologist. Futurologists can never be completely right, and they are often completely wrong – but, hey, they are having a go. A good rule to follow for futurology is that if it sounds believable, it probably won't happen, and if it appears impossible, it might just turn out to be right.

ARROW OF TIME

Scientists don't really know what time is; they just know that it never stops and always goes in one direction, from the past into the future. We are aware of time because of a thing called entropy. This is the way that all things eventually fall apart and spread out. For example, old houses always fall down, but bricks never fall up into houses. Entropy is something the human body must deal with as well.

FUTURE SHOCK

History is always in the past, and we understand it from the records made back then. The Dark Ages 1,500 years ago are so-called because relatively few historical records survive from then. History has been speeding up since people have developed ways to make more records. The world's computers will record more facts about today than all the facts known about the whole of human history up to the day you were born.

There is often a long wait between having the idea for a new technology and the technology itself. For example, people have been talking about driverless cars for so long that it seems surprising we don't see them on the roads yet. However, one day automated vehicles will appear, and then we'll be surprised at how quickly they become normal. This pattern is nothing new; we humans just have difficulty imagining how change happens - but are good at adapting once it does.

BODY AND MACHINE?

Technology has advanced significantly in the last 50 years. Revolutionary changes have been made in both computing and medical sciences. How might these merge in the future so that we can revolutionise our bodies? Should they merge? Before we explore that, lets learn more about the body itself.

HELLO EVERY BODY

Everyone has one, they all work the same way, but each one is unique. If we're going to think about how we might change the human body in the future, we'd better know how the natural body works and what it can do. No other living thing has been studied as closely as the human body. Our bodies are the most complex systems in the universe – and so far we can't find anything cleverer.

LIFE AND DEATH

On average, male humans are born more often than females. For every 100 girls born, 108 boys arrive. However, the average male is slightly more susceptible to fatal health problems and he has a riskier lifestyle, which means that he is more likely to die than the average woman. By the age of 65, for every 100 women there are just 75 men. Globally, the average woman has a life expectancy of 73.5 years, while the average man lives to 68.5.

THE AVERAGE WOMAN

The average human female is about 15 per cent smaller than the average man, but there is a wide range in height and weight. The tallest women live in Latvia, where the average height is 170 cm, while the shortest women are Guatemalans, who average 149 cm. Women in Kuwait have an average BMI (body mass index) of 31.4, while in Bangladesh the average is 19.8. The average woman globally has 2.5 children in her lifetime. Just 50 years ago, the global average was 5 children.

THE AVERAGE MAN

The tallest men live in the Netherlands, where the average height is 183 cm. The shortest men come from East Timor where they grow on average to 160 cm. The fattest men come from Argentina, where the average BMI is 28.7, while in Eritrea, the BMI is 20.1 on average.

All living bodies – and ours are nothing special in this regard – must be able to do eight things to be characterised as alive:

- Move
- Grow
- Remove waste
- Reproduce
- Have an energy source
- Sense the surroundings
- Have a source of raw materials to build the body

WHO'S WHO?

SEX OR GENDER?

The terms 'sex' and 'gender' are often confused. A body's sex is defined by its physical structures, especially the genital organs. The female sex has a vulva and vagina, while the male sex has a penis. There are intersex bodies which have both these organs. Gender refers to a person's social and cultural identity. Usually, a person with a female body adopts the feminine gender, and a person with a male body adopts the masculine gender. This isn't always the case, though. A person born to a female body might identify as the male gender and choose to change their sex to reflect this. Unlike sex, gender roles are loosely defined and subject to change as people choose to live in new ways. How might this change in the future?

WHAT'S WHAT?

BMI

BMI or body mass index is a quick assessment of whether a body is over or under a healthy weight. It's a simple calculation where you divide a person's height by their weight. For adults, a healthy BMI is between 18.5 and 25. Children need to add age and gender to the equation. If a person falls below this range, they are considered underweight. If they are above, they could be considered obese. Both conditions can pose serious health risks.

ON THE SURFACE

The body is covered head to foot in skin – on average, 1.8 square metres of it. Skin is the smartest material around. It is waterproof; super strong, but also soft and flexible; it mends itself; and it can detect contact with other objects. The outer layer, the epidermis, is made of dead, waxy cells which are constantly rubbed away and replaced. The lower layer, the dermis, supplies the epidermis with fresh cells, and has the skin's supply of blood, nerves and touch sensors.

SKIN COLOUR

Epidermis cells contain a brown pigment called melanin which soaks up the invisible and damaging ultraviolet (UV) rays that hit the skin. People who live in locations with a lot of sunshine need more melanin to keep the skin healthy. People from darker, cloudy countries have light skin with less melanin because they need the small amounts of UV in the sunlight to make vitamin D within their skin cells. As a result, humans have a wide range of skin colours.

WHAT'S WHAT?

HUMAN 'RACES'

In the 19th century, a new science called anthropology aimed to study humans as animals. This led to the idea that we all belonged to one of several groups, or 'races'. Races are linked to a region – Africa, Europe, East Asia, etc – and defined by skin colour, face shape and hair type. Biologists use races to describe different populations of animals, but not all species have races. In biological terms, the human species does not have races – it has 'clines'. Clines are gradual changes in features that can be tracked across the whole population. Might new clines develop in the future?

While teens and adults naturally have hair growing on different parts of their body – from facial hair to armpit and pubic hair – many people choose to style this hair or remove it completely. Some even pay lots of money to do so. The amount of hair we have can be dictated by fashion or social movements, which begs the question: if we can remove it, do we really need it? Could we come up with a way to permanently remove this hair or could we stop it from growing in the first place? What if we permanently stopped our body hair from growing, and then discovered we needed it after all?

HAIR COLOUR

As mammals, humans have hair all over the body apart from the palms of the hands, the soles of the feet and the lips. Most of our hair is on our heads. Head hair comes in four general colours made with two pigments, 'eumelanin' and 'pheomelanin'. Red hair has large amounts of pheomelanin, while black hair has large amounts of eumelanin. Blonde hair has small amounts of both pigments, while brown hair has large amounts of both.

Your type of hair depends on the shape of your hair shafts and that depends on the shape of the hair follicle in the skin of the scalp. The cross-section of a straight hair shaft is round, while the curliest hairs are crescent shaped. Wavy hair shafts are egg-shaped.

WHAT'S WHAT?

MALE PATTERN BALDNESS

By the age of 40, half of men will have started to lose their hair. It falls out because some men have hair follicles that can be turned off by certain hormones, like testosterone. What if we could remove or change this type of follicle before baldness sets in?

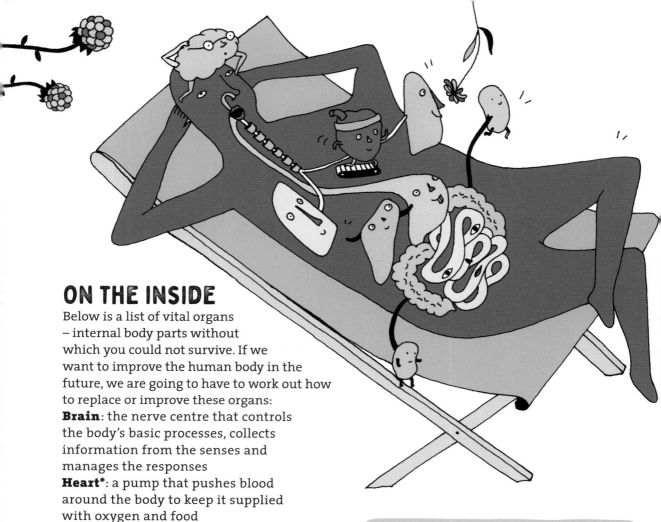

ON THE INSIDE

Below is a list of vital organs – internal body parts without which you could not survive. If we want to improve the human body in the future, we are going to have to work out how to replace or improve these organs:

Brain: the nerve centre that controls the body's basic processes, collects information from the senses and manages the responses

Heart*: a pump that pushes blood around the body to keep it supplied with oxygen and food

Liver: a chemical-processing plant that handles waste and manages the food supply

Stomach and intestines*: the food collection system that reduces food into its simple components so they can be used by the body

Kidneys*: a filtering system that takes the waste out of the blood and turns it into urine (wee) which is flushed out of the body

Lungs*: bags for sucking in air, supplying the blood with oxygen and then puffing the air out again

*The organs marked with * can be replaced by a machine or bypassed with another technology, at least for a short period of time.*

Move over Roboman; the adult human body can bust more moves than you! We have a skeleton with 206 bones. (A baby has 305 but they harden and fuse together as it grows.) The skeleton gives the body shape and provides something solid for 650 muscles to pull against. Your musculoskeletal system is very impressive. The thighbone or femur, the biggest bone, can hold 30 times your body weight, and altogether your joints are capable of 244 separate movements!

SENSES SENSATION

Don't be fooled, we humans have far more than five senses (but there is always room for improvement).

Eyes – light, colour, time: The eyes create images in colour if there's enough light and in black and white when there isn't. They also detect light intensity and track the length of day and night.

Ears – hearing, pressure, motion, gravity, balance: The ears sense pressure waves in the air, which they turn into sound. Ears also pick up changes in air pressure by comparing pressure inside the head with that outside. The fluid-filled parts of the inner ear track the body's motion and position.

Nose – smell: The nose can pick up 10,000 specific chemicals in the air and identify millions of distinct smells made from mixtures of these chemicals. The nose smells dangers (smoke), disease risks (poo and rot) and food quality (ripeness).

Tongue – taste: The tongue picks up five flavours. Sweet means fruit is ripe, whereas sour shows that it is not. Bitter foods are potentially poisonous, while the body can only tolerate a limited saltiness in food. The fifth taste – 'umami' – indicates the protein content of the food.

Touch – pain, heat, cold, pressure, posture, wetness: Five kinds of sensor collect touch information, so you can tell the difference between a gentle stroke to a heavy grip or rapid thump. High-speed touch signals warn of potential hazards – like cuts or heat – and slower pain signals indicate if damage has been done.

The animal kingdom provides plenty of inspiration for adding new senses. Mantis shrimps do not build pictures from three colours like we do, but use six - and they can see ultraviolet light. Pit vipers can detect heat and so see through solid objects. Sharks can pick up electrical signals coming from animal muscles. Dolphins build a picture of their surroundings by echoing sounds off objects. They may even be able to 'see' inside each other's bodies using this system!

SHOULD WE UPGRADE?

The human body is pretty incredible, but it has its flaws. It can be weak, it can be damaged, and it will eventually stop working. If you had the opportunity, would you upgrade yours to be stronger, look better and last longer?

THE EVOLUTION OF YOU

Before we get too busy upgrading the human body, we should know where it came from and how it has improved itself over the years. Theories of human evolution will help us understand why our bodies and minds work the way they do. This is the sort of thing we are going to need to know if we are going to work out how to upgrade them in the future.

PRIMATES

The scientific name for humans is *Homo sapiens*, which translates as 'wise man'. We belong to a group of mammals called primates, which includes monkeys and apes. We share much in common with these animals, and our intelligence arose from primate intelligence. Primates mostly live in trees, where they have to make decisions fast – one false move and they will fall to their death. In addition, forest foods vary from season to season, so primates have good memories and mental maps of their home area, so they can find food all year round.

LEAVING THE FOREST

Humans evolved from African apes that left the forest and set up home in grasslands. Grasslands grow where it is too dry for trees, and so there is a lot less food around – and nowhere to hide. To survive there, an ape would have to be quick thinking, have a good memory, cooperate with others and plan for the future. Is this beginning to sound like anyone?

The striking thing about the human brain is that it has a very large frontal lobe - the bit behind the forehead where we make decisions and dream up plans. The human brain is an extreme example of a monkey brain. By contrast, a shark's brain has a tiny frontal lobe, but huge olfactory bulbs - the bits that process smell picked up in the water. Other animals may have amazing skills, but we primates are built to be quick thinkers.

GIVING US A HAND

Monkeys and apes have hands and feet like you and me with hairless palms and soles that give a strong grip for climbing. The inside toes or fingers are opposable, meaning they work like a pincer with the other fingers. In humans, this resulted in a flexible thumb that can touch the other fingers (no other ape can do this). So the human hand can create a strong fist-like grip as well as a fine fingertip grip. They both come in handy.

Much like other land mammals, human fingers and toes have a thickened tip - a nail - made from keratin. The nail protects the finger; it can crack, and regrow, so the fingertip is not damaged all the time. This is an example of how the body evolved to protect itself. Now long nails without cracks, or painted interesting colours, show that our lifestyles have evolved to no longer include hard manual work. In other words, we've won the game of life (or have we?).

WHO'S WHO?

LUCY

Standing about 110 cm tall, Lucy's 3.2 million-year-old fossil skeleton was found in 1974 in Ethiopia – and named after a Beatles' song playing on the camp stereo at the time. Lucy was the first fossil specimen of an ape that walked on two legs. The first human species evolved from apes like Lucy around 2.5 million years ago. Modern humans, *Homo sapiens*, appeared in East Africa, around 300,000 years ago.

WALKING ON TWO LEGS

Humans are the only bipedal walking mammal, meaning we stand on two legs. Kangaroos are bipedal too, but they can't walk, just hop. Bipedality means we are slowcoaches compared to other mammals, so why do we do it? It helps us see into the distance. It makes it easier to reach fruits and nuts from high bushes. Plus it frees up our hands for holding food, babies and tools. All of these things have contributed to humans becoming a powerful species.

BORN EARLY

Walking on two legs gave humans a problem. Their pelvis bones had to be thick enough to hold the strong core muscles that keep humans upright. That meant less room for babies to pass through the mother's pelvis when they were born. Babies were born earlier than other mammals so they were still small enough to fit, but they were less developed and so helpless that their parents must care for them for several years. Is this an advantage for humans?

One of the earliest human species was *Homo habilis*, or 'handy man'. These little guys (around 130 cm tall) lived 2 million years ago and were named for the tools they made. The tool design was passed down the generations for three quarters of a million years, until *Homo erectus*, a taller, tougher species took over. Advances in tool tech took hundreds of thousands of years to develop back then. Can you imagine developing technology that slowly now?

BIG HEADS

As mammals develop during pregnancy, the head and brain develop first. A newborn has a large head in relation to the size of its body compared to an adult. Therefore human babies that evolved to be born earlier were born with bigger heads and bigger brains than their ape cousins. So it is likely that the things that make us human – big brains, bipedality and nimble hands – all evolved because of each other!

The 'Homo' part of our scientific name refers to a genus, or group of human species. The genus's name means 'human' in Latin. It is pronounced hoh-moh. Don't get confused with the term 'homo', pronounced ho-moh, which is Greek for 'same'. The exact number of human species is always being debated but there were at least ten, living all over Africa, Asia and Europe. We are the only ones that survive today. As little as 30,000 years ago, *Homo sapiens* was sharing the planet with other human species.

WHAT'S WHAT?

CRYPTIC OESTRUS

Adult female humans have 'cryptic oestrus', which means that a woman's fertility is hidden from others. It is very rare for animals to do this. Most give out a signal – such as a change in smell or genitals that swell and turn bright pink! – to tell males that she is ovulating and so now is the time for a successful mating. Why humans should hide this information from each other is one of the most intriguing questions in human evolution.

SOCIAL NETWORK

Our nearest living relatives, the bonobos of Central Africa, live in forests in troops of about 50 apes. Any fewer and the troop has difficulty defending its territory from neighbouring ones. Any bigger and the group splits into rival factions. A human social group is about three times this size – about 150 people. It was harder for humans to survive on grasslands than for bonobos in the forest, and so ancient humans worked together in bigger groups to stay alive. Bonobos and other apes build a sense of community by hugging, touching and grooming each other's fur. A human society forges bonds using language. It is good to talk – and much quicker than grooming.

Human conversation is often 'small talk', where people check if everyone is OK, exchange news and gossip. That worked well in prehistoric communities, but in modern society we often meet strangers. What do we talk about? Our culture has invented celebrities to solve this problem. Celebs are people that we can gossip about without having ever met them.

IMAGINATION

As well as forging social bonds, language allows humans to describe things that haven't happened yet and make up stories about things that can never happen. Whether language came before imagination or the other way around is a question that is hard to answer. Evidence from ancient settlements shows that around 40,000 years ago there was an explosion of cave art, jewellery making and technological innovations. Does this show when humans developed an imagination?

Everyone loves a good story. It's easy to imagine our ancient ancestors clustered around the fire after a hard day gathering nuts, clubbing bison and avoiding sabre-toothed cats to listen to stories about great heroes and terrible demons. Humans are the only animals that make stuff up like this, and even though we know stories are not true or are not happening to us right now they can still make us feel happy, sad, frightened and angry. What's that all about?

WHO'S WHO?

CARL JUNG

About 100 years ago, this Swiss psychoanalyst came up with the idea that human personalities are formed from what he called a 'collective consciousness'. He believed we all developed our particular personality during our childhoods by responding to the same set of characters we heard about in stories and saw in art. He called them archetypes, and they include terrible monsters coming to get us, heroes who save us and carers who look after us.

EMOTIONS

The idea of looking at apes to understand ourselves sprang from the work of Charles Darwin. He is most famous for the theory of natural selection, which explains how species evolve from ancestors, but one of his most interesting books was about emotion. He suggested emotions are a short-cut system that prepare an animal for a particular situation. For example, anger makes the animal ready to fight, while sadness ensures that other members of the social group offer help and protection.

WHEN DID WE BECOME HUMAN?

It's clear that humans are special (even if we do say so ourselves). Did this special human nature appear suddenly at some point or has it been gradually growing and changing? How will it develop in the future? And what will being human mean?

INTELLIGENCE

We humans always tell ourselves that we are the cleverest animals on the planet – there, I just did it again. Although we can never know what another animal is thinking, we can be pretty sure that we are the brainiest beasts around. I mean, no other species produces books like this one! But what exactly is intelligence? How is it measured and how can we enhance it in the future?

IQ TESTING

The most well-known intelligence test is the IQ, or intelligence quotient, test. This test was developed at the start of the 20th century. French researcher Alfred Binet designed a test of symbols and visual puzzles for children to take before they learned to read. In those days, only some children got proper schooling and once that process started it would be impossible to compare intelligences. A decade later, an adult form of the test was created. Compared to other psychological measurements, IQ tests are very reliable, so we can use them to show whether our efforts to get cleverer are working or not.

WAYS OF LEARNING

You have been learning in different ways – sometimes automatically – since the moment you were born.

Habituation: This is when the body learns to be less sensitive to an event. For example, on her first day at a bell factory, Wendy jumped every time she heard the clang of a bell being tested. After a week, she became habituated to the noise and no longer noticed it.

Conditioning: This kind of learning is based on associations with a stimulus. After a month at the bell factory, Wendy's boss decided that all the bells made each morning would be tested just before everyone took their lunch break. After several days of this, Wendy became conditioned to feel hungry when she heard the bells go off.

Active learning: Wendy decided she didn't like working at the bell factory anymore, and so she took a course in earplug manufacturing. To pass, she needed to learn actively by deliberately paying attention to the teacher and being aware of which bits she understood and which bits she didn't.

In the century since IQ tests were introduced, the world's average IQ has gone up. Each test is designed to give an average score of 100, and when researchers design new tests every few years, they need to make them slightly harder than before to keep the average. Perhaps people are more used to solving cognitive problems now; perhaps it's down to a better diet or fewer diseases; it might simply be that we live in a more stimulating world and that drives up our mental abilities.

KNOWLEDGE

Intelligence requires a general knowledge that everyone is expected to have, as well as expert knowledge that relates to a job or hobby. However, knowledge that would have been thought of as expert a few generations ago, such as being able to read or do maths, is now regarded as general knowledge. Will this shift from expert to general continue, or will it go into reverse?

ARE THERE MANY TYPES OF INTELLIGENCE?

Is human intelligence one thing? Or is it really a collection of different abilities which we try to group together to make it easier to measure? Can we consider a wide range of abilities, such as musicality or sports skills, as different types of intelligence?

IN THE MIND

There's one very important bit of the human body that can't be shown on anatomical diagrams – your mind. Some ancient people believed that thoughts, dreams and emotions came from the heart. But use your head: do you think that is true? You probably agree with scientific evidence that the mind is created by the brain – but science still struggles to get inside our heads to work out how the mind is made and how to compare my mental world with yours. Any thoughts?

I THINK, THEREFORE I AM

In 1619, French philosopher René Descartes woke from a dream. Then he woke up again and realised the first waking had been a dream. Descartes was very confused and began to wonder if he really was awake now. He reasoned that someone who wasn't truly awake wouldn't have these doubts. The very act of thinking about his existence meant he must exist as a conscious being. He thought, therefore he was. And so am I – but I'm not sure about you.

THEORY OF MIND

Have you played hide and seek with a toddler? You'd definitely win. Little children hide by covering their eyes – if they can't see anything, they think they can't be seen. They have no 'theory of mind', which is the idea that your thoughts and perceptions are not the same as the thoughts and perceptions of someone else. Children don't learn this until they are around four, and scientists disagree about whether other animals have a theory of mind at all.

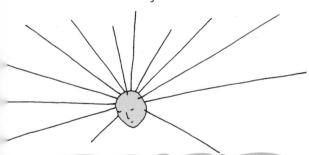

The theory of mind reveals that we can never really experience the world as another person does. In the 1990s, neurologists discovered brain cells called 'mirror neurons'. These cells fire when you do a thing, such as kick a ball, and they also fire when you see someone else kick a ball. Mirror neurons seem to create a link between our experiences and those of others, helping us to empathise with other people.

A HARD PROBLEM

You and I both know that the sky is blue. However, is your experience of blue – what mind experts call its 'qualia' – the same as mine? I can never see blue as you do. If I did, I might find that your experience of it is my experience of green. Without being able to compare qualia, scientists can't tell us where they come from. This is the so-called hard problem of consciousness – and it's really tricky stuff.

WHAT ARE ANIMALS THINKING?

Do you think that animals have the same level of consciousness as us? Most people nowadays believe that animals are conscious and have feelings, but how can we be sure? If an animal did think like us, would that make it 'human' too?

SLEEP

Sleep requires no explanation. We all do it – some of you may be thinking about it now. But you might be surprised to learn that while all animals sleep, no one knows why. If we can work out this mystery it could have one of two benefits: We learn a way to live without sleep and make more use of our time, or we learn why sleep is needed by the brain or body, which will in turn help us live in a healthier way.

Sleep researchers collect data while their subject sleeps, using an EEG or 'electroencephelograph'. Nerve cells produce electrical pulses, and an EEG measures the electric field created around the head by the brain's activity. The field flickers on and off at various frequencies, forming what are called brain waves. When we are awake but relaxed, the brain makes alpha waves. Beta waves form when we are thinking hard, while delta waves show we are in a deep sleep.

THE SLEEP STATE

When you are asleep your body becomes inactive and your mind enters a state of low arousal. As you drop off, your muscles relax and physiological functions slow, your breathing and heart rates drop, and your body temperature dips. Your awareness level drops below consciousness, but the state is not quite like being knocked out because your senses have not shut down completely – a loud noise or strong touch will wake you up.

DREAMS

The body goes through a cycle every 90 minutes as it sleeps, first getting deeper and deeper into sleep, and then rousing into a state called REM, or rapid eye movement. During REM sleep, you dream and the mind fires up so you can experience weird stories (or perhaps mundane ones). Not everyone remembers what happened in their dreams, and some people cannot even remember dreaming, but everyone does it.

Some people see dreams as symbolic of the subconscious mind, where we hide our deepest fears and desires. Others suggest that a dream is a story constructed from random signals leaking across from activity in other parts of the brain. Yet another idea is that a dream is associated with the brain processing the memories collected the day before. The truth is no one knows what dreams are.

WHAT'S WHAT?

YAWNING

Why do we yawn? Is it a way of flushing the body with oxygen to keep the body alert as sleepiness takes over? Or is it a signal to others that it is time for everyone to huddle up and sleep – assuming our ancestors slept in groups? This tiresome activity is yet another sleep mystery.

A REASON TO SLEEP

We always feel better after a good night's sleep but that isn't really because we have been resting. While asleep, the body uses 95 per cent of the energy it uses while awake but inactive. A lack of sleep does stop the body functioning so well, especially the immune system, so undoubtedly sleep helps the body repair and protect itself. The question is, why do we have to be unconscious for that to happen?

WOULD YOU WANT TO STAY AWAKE?

If you could find a way of living without sleep, would you do so? Would you miss having dreams? What would you do with all the extra time? You should be able to do all your studying and still have time for a lot of fun. You'd need more than three meals a day, though. What would the fourth meal be called?

MAKING MEMORIES

A thousand years ago, the philosopher Aristotle believed information from the eyes, ears and other senses were combined at the front of the brain into 'common sense'. Common sense guided our instincts as to what to do – kill it, eat it, run away from it – then moved information to the back of the brain where it was stored as a memory. We now have a better idea of how memories are formed and organised, but we're still in the dark about where it all happens.

SENSORY MEMORY

All memories begin as perceptions of the world around us arriving via our different senses. They enter our consciousness in the 'sensory memory'. Studies show that they stay in this system for less than a second and that it can hold around twelve perceptions. The items that catch our attention then move to the short-term, or working memory, which is thought to be located at the front of the brain.

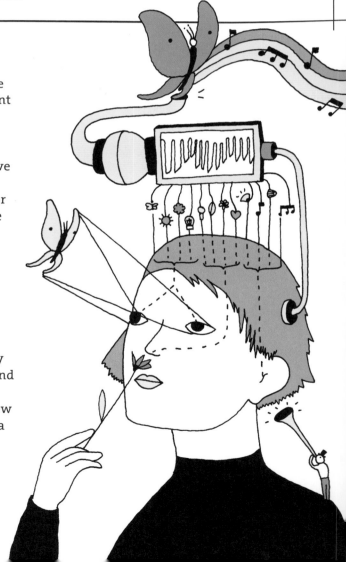

WORKING MEMORY

This memory system was also known as the 'telephonic memory' because it can hold something about as complex as a telephone number. The working memory will hold on to this information for around fifteen seconds. Then it begins to fade away, as the sensory memory offers it new things for consideration. You can renew a short-term memory by repeating it over and over in your head.

LONG-TERM MEMORY

Once a short-term memory fades away and is replaced with a new one, you can never get it back. Only memories that have been transferred to the long-term memory can be recalled over and over. Facts, figures and events are called declarative memories, and they are stored in the explicit memory. Physical skills, such as how to play computer games or the piano, are called procedural memories. They are stored long-term in the implicit memory.

WHAT'S WHAT?

ENGRAMS

It is believed that memories are stored as networks of nerve cells called 'engrams' (although this has yet to be proved). Strong memories that are recalled often or had a significant impact maintain larger engrams than unimportant memories, which you seldom think about. Brain scientists like to say, "Cells that fire together, wire together." So if you don't use an engram, it will fade away over time – and the memory it held will be forgotten.

The implicit memory is closely linked to the cerebellum, which means 'little brain'. This is the folded region under the main brain at the back. The cerebellum's nerve cells are arranged in layers, which wire together to form circuits that control the body's movements. A procedural memory is stored here, containing everything you do without having to think about it. Self-programming neural networks used by artificial intelligence often have the same kind of set-up as the self-programming cerebellum.

The explicit memory divides its memories in two. The first group are 'episodic memories', which record the events of your life. You'll remember several insignificant things about yesterday, and these will slowly be replaced in the future, but the big moments will last much longer. The second memory groups are 'semantic' ones, which are general knowledge about the world.

IS PERFECT MEMORY A GOOD THING?

If you could train your memory so that you remembered everything, would that be good or bad? You would be able to pass all your exams easily, but you would also never forget anything painful or embarrassing. Would it be worth it?

PERSONAL IDENTITY

Who are you? I don't mean what's your name, but rather what makes you, you, and not someone else. Simply, we are all a combination of memories and perceptions, and that combination is always changing. Who we are today is not who we will be in 10 years' time. So if our identity is constantly changing naturally, how do we keep track of it when we consider things like cloning and mind uploading?

Since ancient times, philosophers have wondered if babies are born knowing anything. Our memory of our very early life is more or less non-existent, but that does not mean we did not know things at that time. However, it is generally accepted that the human mind starts as a 'tabula rasa', or a blank sheet, and that every thought and memory comes from what a person experiences as they go through life.

EXISTENCE AND AUTHENTICITY

Let's play a mind game to help us think about personal identity. Imagine a teleportation machine that can beam you to Mars. You step in and dematerialise, and your information is sent to the red planet – it will take a few minutes to get there. Where are you in this time? Your body does not exist, and presumably neither does your mind. Without a body or mind you no longer have a personal identity. Instead you exist solely in the memories and records of others. The machine then recreates you on Mars. It has copied every aspect of your body on Earth from the subatomic level up, but using different atoms. Are you still the same person? Your mind and memories are all intact and as far as you are concerned, you cannot tell the difference. However, something has gone wrong. The machine glitched and made two of you – both perfect copies of your original body, and thus identical. Which one is the real you?

PERSONALITY

Personalities are easy enough to recognise and describe, but it is another thing to measure them, and even trickier to explain where they came from. One system defines personality using five traits:

Openness: how curious are you about new experiences

Conscientiousness: how disciplined and organised are you

Outgoingness: whether you like being with people or prefer to be alone

Agreeableness: whether you prefer to be friendly or if getting your way is more important

Sensitivity: how often you get very emotional and stressed

It is possible to show that personality traits run in families. Is that because they are inherited along with hair colour and other features, or is it because we learn how to behave from our parents (who learned it from theirs...)?

EXPERIENCE

The two versions of you are only identical in the moment of their creation. Straight afterwards they begin living separate lives, form different memories and thus have taken on different identities. This thought experiment illustrates how our own identity shifts as we go through life. The person you are now will not exist in 20 years. (What about in 70 years or in a thousand? Future you might live a long time; we'll take a look at that later.)

IS THERE A 'REAL' YOU?

You probably won't notice the changes, but your identity is always shifting and who you are now will not exist for as long as you do. How does that make you feel?

LIVING TOGETHER

The latest thinking is that our species, *Homo sapiens*, appeared around 200,000 years ago in East Africa – although some evidence puts it at 350,000 years ago. For most of that time, our prehistoric ancestors were a small group of African apes, living in bands of about 150 individuals. Now we live in groups made up of millions and reside on all Earth's continents. How did that happen and, if we continue to develop at the same rate, how might we be living in the future?

WHO'S IN CHARGE?

Our closest living relatives, the bonobos, live in communities with a single leader. How did they get to be boss? A despotic chimp leader, one who is always using violence to get other apes to do his bidding – it's always a male – doesn't last long. A more successful leader offers support and protection to friendly members of his troop. When his position is challenged, he becomes very sad, so all his friends offer their support – and any challenger slinks away.

MIGRATION

Around 70,000 years ago, ancient humans left Africa and followed the south Asian coast, before arriving in Australia around 65,000 years ago. Around 45,000 years ago, modern humans spread into Europe and northern Asia, and 16,000 years ago, they crossed from Siberia to the Americas. In just the last 1,000 years, we have reached Iceland and New Zealand. In the 1950s, permanent Antarctic settlements were set up, and since 2001, at least two humans have been orbiting in space at any one time. Where next?

Migrating humans shared Europe and Asia with other human species, such as the Neanderthals. By 37,000 years ago these cousin humans had all disappeared. Did we wipe them out in war, eat their food so they starved or did we interbreed? Probably all three. People with a non-African heritage carry two per cent Neanderthal genes.

EMILIO MARCOS PALMA

In 1978, Emilio was born in the Argentinian town of Esperanza. Why's his birth such a big deal? Esperanza is a town on the Antarctic Peninsula, and baby Emilio was the first person to be born on the ice continent, the most southern birth in history. To date, ten more Antarcticans have been born.

BEING DISGUSTING

Disgust is the only learned emotion; all the others are instinctive. Disgust is designed to protect the body. For example, it helps us avoid foods contaminated with dangerous things like rot, poo, blood or maggots. However, humans also use disgust for social protection. Every society has taboos, or banned behaviours, but they are subject to change. Some behaviours which were considered taboos fifty years ago are now accepted. What taboos do you recognise now? Could you imagine these being accepted one day?

One idea that helps to explain human evolution is that our bodies have become more childlike as our environment has become less threatening. A newborn baby is similar in development to a chimp several weeks before it is born. It could be said that the way we behave towards each other is more childlike as well. Adult chimps will try to kill any stranger, but adult humans are as trusting of strangers as baby chimps. This difference means humans can live relatively peacefully in cities that are home to millions.

FEEDING THE PEOPLE

Before humans spread out from Africa, it is estimated that our species could have numbered just 1,000 people. Around 10,000 years ago, when humans first began to grow their own food supply, the global population of humans was estimated as being about a million. With a constant supply of food, that population started to grow, and in 1804, the number of humans hit a billion (a thousand million). By 2012, it was 7 billion, and we are nearly at 8 billion today.

THE MALTHUSIAN CATASTROPHE

In 1798, English historian Thomas Malthus calculated that the human population was growing much faster than the growth of food production needed to feed everyone. He believed the human population would soon collapse in a catastrophic famine. Since then, the human population has increased more than eight-fold. Malthus's ideas weren't wrong, but he didn't foresee the chemical fertilisers we would invent to boost the amount of food we can get from land. Today, a third of the human population survives on food that only grows thanks to chemicals made in factories.

Ecologists, the scientists who study how organisms survive together in habitats, use the idea of 'carrying capacity' to decide how many members of a species can survive in a location. For example, a forest habitat could support hundreds of squirrels but only a couple of bears. Agriculture is a way of hugely increasing the carrying capacity of land, by replacing a diverse community of wildlife with a single crop plant.

WHO'S WHO?

FRITZ HABER

In 1908, this German chemist worked out a way of turning nitrogen (the most common gas in the air) into chemicals for making fertilisers. This discovery transformed global agriculture and ensured that we can produce enough plant food for a human population even bigger than today's. Unfortunately Haber's chemical process also made it much easier to produce bombs – just in time for World War I!

POPULATION CONTROL

Populations can grow by either new children being added or older people not dying. For the last 25 years, the number of children being born each day has not really changed, but the number of people dying per day has gone down, and so the world's population is going up. If the birth rate stays about the same, the human population will top out at around 11 billion in the second half of this century.

WHAT'S WHAT?

THE ONE-CHILD POLICY

China has a population of 1.4 billion people – almost one in five of all humans. To reduce population growth, between 1979 and 2015, the Chinese government asked people to have just one child. The policy didn't reduce China's population because death rates also went down. In addition it led to the 4-2-1 problem, where four grandparents and two parents all rely on the support of one child as they get too old to work.

RIP

ARE THERE TOO MANY HUMANS?

Is the number of humans on Earth a quantity that needs controlling? If so how do you control it? Is it possible to decide which humans are surplus to requirements?

WEALTH AND STATUS

Adam Smith, the Scottish philosopher who started the study of economics, had a clever definition about humans: "Man," he said, "is an animal that makes bargains." There are actually several animals that trade with each other, but only we humans have created a system where we can buy and sell things with anyone anywhere on Earth. Smith's real point was that this system arose because of our drive to gather wealth. Why do we do that?

WHAT IS WEALTH?

Once a society can produce more food than it can eat, it becomes possible for people to do other work, such as making things or providing services. They can then exchange this work for food, or money to buy food or for services from other workers. This system allows people to amass assets (money, food or other things) that protect them against problems in the future. However, the drive for wealth in human society continues far beyond the need for survival. Why is that?

SEEKING STATUS

All complex animal groups have hierarchies, where individuals have a certain social rank. In animal societies, these ranks are based on the drive to survive and reproduce, but in human groups it's more complex. Our social status has an impact on the way other people treat us, and that affects our happiness. Wealth is the most common signal of social status – but don't worry, there are others.

ETIQUETTE

The proper name for manners is 'etiquette', which is a set of rules about what to do in different social situations. In the past, not knowing the correct etiquette showed that you were from a different social status. Today these rules aren't followed as much.

WHAT'S WHAT?

BLING

Why are gold and diamonds so valuable? For one thing, they are rare, so not everyone can own them. Secondly, they are pretty. Thirdly, diamonds and gold will never corrode or crumble into dust. Your gold and gems will be just as bling after you die, so the generations to come can hold on to your wealth.

Wealthy people are high status because of what they own. Humans tend to compare themselves to those around them. Having the same things as your friends indicates equal status. When a group member gets something new, their status might go up. However, there are other ways of judging status, like being 'cool'. Some social groups base their status on how religious people are, how educated or expert they are, or how much they help others.

SHOULD WEALTH BE EQUAL?

Would your prefer to live in a society where everyone had about the same wealth or one where some had much more than others? How would you control individual wealth and would that have an impact on everyone's wealth as a whole?

According to the law, you are a unique person. As a distinct individual you have rights, such as the right to possessions and to be in charge of your body. You are also responsible for what you choose to do – good and bad. Most of us also want to belong to a group and to form relationships. As a result we present a version of ourselves that is individual but also shows which group we belong to.

CLOTHES

The most significant aspect of our look is clothing. People probably started to clothe themselves to keep out the cold and protect against the sun. Since prehistoric times, clothing has also been used for modesty, a way of keeping sexual features hidden from strangers. Formal clothing, such as a suit or a uniform, conforms to a set of colours and styles that makes everyone look the same. By contrast, at a party, people wear brighter, more varied clothing to show their individuality.

Using cosmetics, or make-up, on the face has a long history. For example, ancient Egyptians of both sexes, smeared a dark powder (kohl) around their eyes. This was probably, at first at least, to absorb the glare of the Sun.

MAKE-UP

The human face is central to our identity. Our brain is hard-wired to recognise faces, so we often see them everywhere – like in the Moon or on burnt toast. The majority of western women under 35 wear some make-up but, as women get older, this number decreases. The number of men using make-up is increasing, but is still comparatively low. Make-up is as important to a person's public persona as clothing.

FASHION

You already have formal clothing for work or school and other clothes that are more 'you' – but now you need new stuff because your old clothes aren't in fashion! Finding something new that no one else has yet offers us an opportunity to reinforce our social status. Others copy the new look (in their own way, of course). What counts for normal clothing gradually changes – and the old styles go out of fashion.

Shoes changed the way we walk. Fossil evidence shows that our toe bones have become less thick since we started wearing shoes around 40,000 years ago. Early shoes protected the soles of our feet from sharp objects but were pretty flimsy. Until sturdy modern shoes arrived in the 1800s, people walked in a more flat-footed way, poking their toes forward. Modern shoes protect the feet so we make longer, faster strides. How will we walk in the future?

WHAT'S WHAT?

AN INFLUENCER

Businesses today tell people about their products through 'influencers' on social media. An influencer is a celebrity. Celebrities are in our social group because we know and talk about them, even though we've never met. They have high social status; they're wealthy and cool, so we want to buy the stuff that they have.

TATTOOS

Tattooing has been used for millennia in various locations, but it was spread around the world by sailors over the last 400 years. They got the idea from the Pacific islands, where tattoos were symbols of social status. Today many people see tattoos as a permanent personal artwork that indicates individuality and adulthood. In a tattoo, inks are injected through tiny cuts to create a permanently coloured layer under the skin.

PIERCINGS

This common form of body modification involves making a hole in the skin for an implant – a ring, bar or stud. Ear piercing is an ancient practice that happens all over the world. It is relatively easy to pierce the fleshy earlobe, but other soft body parts can be pierced too. Once the implant is removed, small piercings will close up, perhaps leaving a small scar. However, larger piercings form a 'fistula', or permanent hole in the skin.

FOOT BINDING

Until the 1930s Chinese baby girls' feet were tightly bound in cloth to stop the bones growing. Tiny mangled feet – hidden in 'cute' little shoes – meant a woman could only walk in very small steps making her relatively helpless. This was a signal that she belonged to a wealthy high-status family that could afford servants.

A hairstyle is a medium-term change in look – it will still be here tomorrow but you can grow it out and try something new in a few months. The history and culture of hairstyles is an enormous subject. Some cultures cut head hair off, others cover it in scarves or wigs, while the Long-horn Miao people of southern China make elaborate headpieces out of great swathes of their ancestors' hair!

EXTREME BODY MODS

Some body modifications seem extreme to us, but are traditional in other cultures. Sometimes, a person might modify their body in an extreme way because it is unusual in their own society, and they don't want to conform. Examples include:

Filing the front teeth into a point.

Tooth blackening, which permanently stains the teeth. This is traditional in some parts of Southeast Asia.

Neck rings, where stiff metal rings are fitted around the neck when young, and new ones are fitted regularly, pushing down on the shoulder bones to give the impression of a long neck. This is a traditional practice in Myanmar.

Scarification, where permanent patterns are formed by scars on the skin. This is a tradition from some African cultures, as well as others.

Eye implants, which place tiny shapes in the outer layer of the eye as a cosmetic enhancement. This new practice began in the Netherlands in 2002, but isn't legal everywhere.

Extreme body modification is risky. It can cause ill health, perhaps long term, and there is no changing your mind if you do not like the result.

WHAT'S THE FUTURE OF BODY MODIFICATION?

Today, body modifications are mostly highly personal and artistic, but in the future we may be able to merge these techniques with computer technology. What kinds of tech body mods can you think of?

MEDICAL POWERS

So far, we've thought about the natural state of the human body, how we understand ourselves as animals and how that might allow us to change in the future. The process of evolution that created humans is built on the fact that some animals live well and others die – that's just natural. But medical science uses technology to free us from pain and suffering for as long as possible. That's not strictly 'natural', but we would not have it any other way.

CHEMICAL MEDICINES

When a gorilla gets a stomach ache, it eats the leaves of certain plants that help to kill stomach bugs. Human medicines arose from plants used in traditional potions. Today, pharmacologists, the scientists who make medicines, understand how certain plant chemicals work to cure a disease. Generally it is due to the drug's shape locking on to the body chemicals involved. Future drug research will work out the chemical processes that cause diseases and build drugs to inhibit them.

Since the invention of the X-ray machine over 100 years ago, seeing inside the body without cutting it open has revolutionised medicine. Today, the cutting edge of medical imaging is fMRI, which stands for functional magnetic resonance imaging. The system uses a magnet that turns the body into a radio transmitter and the signal it gives out makes a picture of the insides. Chemicals added to the blood show the body at work. This is particularly useful for watching the brain as it thinks, sees or even dreams.

SURGERY

You could think of surgery as the ultimate in body modification, since surgeons cut away damaged body parts or add bolts and plates to fix injuries. In the future, robots will perform surgery, although they won't replace human doctors. A robot surgeon can perform minute cuts more precise than even the most skilled human, and that will speed up healing time. Surgeons already use robots to perform delicate keyhole surgery, where a robot's precision is most useful.

WHAT'S THE MATTER?

A doctor's first job is to diagnose you. You tell them what is wrong and they ask questions and examine you to narrow down the list of possible problems to the most likely ones. Will we always get medical treatment this way? Perhaps an expert computer system will be able to do it instead, using a sequence of questions and scanners that examine the inside and outside of the body.

WHAT'S WHAT?

GENERAL ANAESTHETICS

During surgery, doctors use drugs called anaesthetics to cut the connections between the brain and the nervous system, making you fall into unconsciousness. How anaesthetics do this is a mystery. If we could find out, that might help us understand how the brain creates our consciousness, and then we might learn to recreate consciousness in a computer.

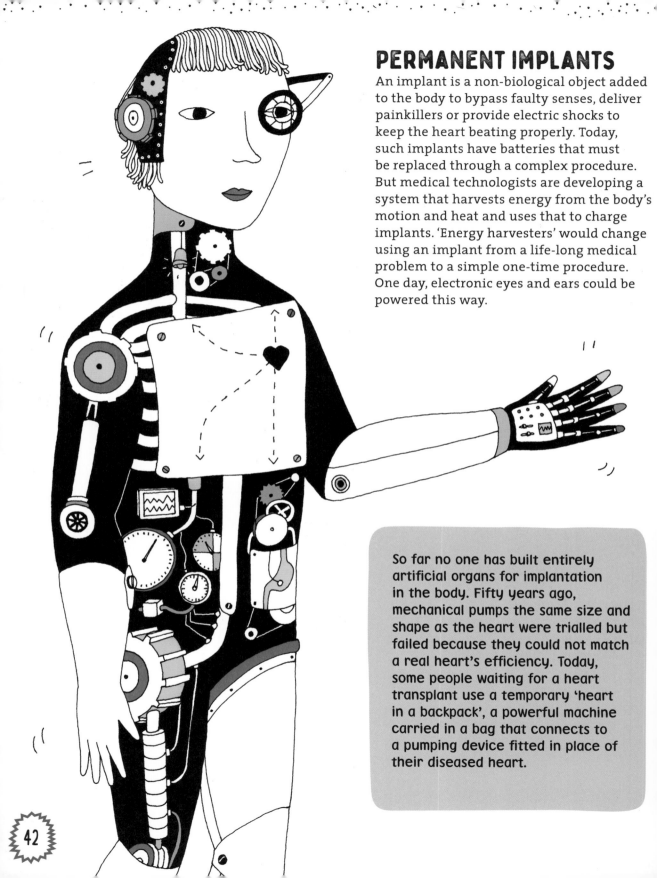

PERMANENT IMPLANTS

An implant is a non-biological object added to the body to bypass faulty senses, deliver painkillers or provide electric shocks to keep the heart beating properly. Today, such implants have batteries that must be replaced through a complex procedure. But medical technologists are developing a system that harvests energy from the body's motion and heat and uses that to charge implants. 'Energy harvesters' would change using an implant from a life-long medical problem to a simple one-time procedure. One day, electronic eyes and ears could be powered this way.

So far no one has built entirely artificial organs for implantation in the body. Fifty years ago, mechanical pumps the same size and shape as the heart were trialled but failed because they could not match a real heart's efficiency. Today, some people waiting for a heart transplant use a temporary 'heart in a backpack', a powerful machine carried in a bag that connects to a pumping device fitted in place of their diseased heart.

The history of replacing missing body parts is surprisingly long. For example, an ancient Egyptian mummy from 3,500 years ago had a wooden toe buckled to the foot and US president George Washington had dentures made from hippo teeth.

PAIN

Pain is created by nerve cells called nociceptors, which send warning signals to the brain when body parts around them are damaged. When the pain has gone, the body has healed. A painkiller drug interferes with this process, either at the nociceptor or in the brain. All animals have nociceptors and respond to injuries. Is this a reflex action or do they perceive pain like we do?

PROSTHESES

Today's prosthetic limbs are much smarter than simple wooden legs or hooks in place of a hand. Users control different robotic actions – like a false hand gripping – by tensing muscles where the body connects to the prosthetic. Prosthetic leg joints detect motion and replicate natural movements at the knee and ankle automatically to help with walking. A future goal of prosthetic engineering is to create a brain interface, so false limbs are controlled by thoughts.

VIRTUAL REALITY

Virtual reality technology not only allows surgeons to have a good look around inside your body to plan an operation – it can also help patients. People who have lost control of their limbs in a stroke, or other brain injury, find it easier to learn to use them again in a VR world. This turns treatment into a game. One day, VR might replace the body altogether – more on that later.

IF IT'S NOT BROKEN, WHY FIX IT?

As medical science seeks to save lives, it develops ways to replace entire body parts. As this technology gets better it may be able to improve on the natural body. Should doctors be allowed to replace a person's healthy body parts with artificial ones?

COSMETIC PROCEDURES

What are you willing to do to look good? Medical procedures developed to reconstruct the body or treat serious disfigurements have been repurposed for a wider set of cosmetic uses, which all fall into someone's idea of 'looking good'. Cosmetic procedures are becoming less expensive and more common, and they are seen as a normal thing to do in some communities. The next question might be: When is looking good, good enough?

PLASTIC PROCEDURES

There are about 9 million cosmetic surgeries in the world every year, and that number is increasing. The top countries for cosmetic surgery are the United States, Brazil, Mexico and Germany. More than 80 per cent of the patients are women and the most common procedure is breast enlargement. Other common procedures reshape noses, remove wrinkles around the eyes (facelifts) and remove fat (liposuction).

BOTOX

The most common non-surgical cosmetic procedures are botox injections. Botox is short for 'Botulinum toxin', a powerful poison that blocks the connection between nerves and muscles. Tiny amounts paralyse facial muscles for a few months, making the skin appear smooth and wrinkle free – especially around the eyes and forehead. Botox injections are not to be taken lightly; if the toxin enters the wrong muscle group it can paralyse the wrong part of the face.

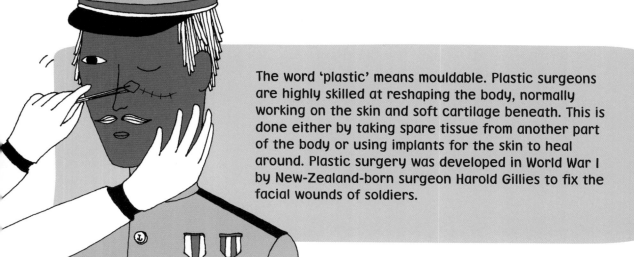

The word 'plastic' means mouldable. Plastic surgeons are highly skilled at reshaping the body, normally working on the skin and soft cartilage beneath. This is done either by taking spare tissue from another part of the body or using implants for the skin to heal around. Plastic surgery was developed in World War I by New-Zealand-born surgeon Harold Gillies to fix the facial wounds of soldiers.

Cosmetic surgery is not risk free. The deeper a surgeon has to cut, the more risky the operation. For example, some bum implants are so dangerous that they are now illegal. Also, as the demand for cosmetic procedures increases, poorly trained surgeons are offering cheap services. That is increasing the number of errors that create permanent damage which even an expert plastic surgeon cannot fix.

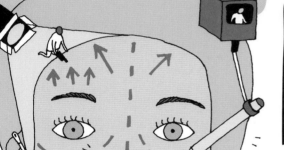

WHO'S WHO?

SUSHRUTA

This Indian doctor from 2,700 years ago was the first recorded surgeon. He designed all kinds of surgical implements, described hundreds of plants and minerals used as medicines and developed many techniques – including using the bites of soldier ants to stitch wounds! Sushruta is said to have performed the first nose job, rebuilding an injured nose from skin cut from the cheeks.

WHAT'S WHAT?

FILLERS

The shape of the lips or cheeks can be changed by pumping in liquid fillers. The effects of natural fillers like collagen proteins and fats only last a few months. If they go wrong they grow out eventually like a bad haircut. Permanent fillers contain gels and plastic beads. If these go wrong you just have to live with it.

WILL WE ALL BE PLASTIC?

The way famous people look has always had a big influence on the way the rest of us see ourselves. If all famous people have cosmetic fillers and botox, will that become the norm for the rest of us? What if you don't like that look? Or can't afford it?

SMART AND STUPID DRUGS

The word 'drug' can mean different things. A doctor will administer life-saving drugs to patients. These drugs are known as medicine. But drugs are also chemicals that change how we behave and feel. Some drugs are legal; some are illegal; some stop us from over-thinking things, while others help us think more.

DESIGNER DRUGS

Illegal drugs like cocaine and heroin are natural products made from plants that have been used as medicines for centuries. In the future, it is likely that chemists will create so-called 'designer drugs'; artificial chemicals with the same effects as natural drugs, but which aren't yet illegal. Many countries are tackling this problem by listing legal drugs and making every other chemical illegal. Designer drugs have an extra danger. As well as overdose problems, the criminal labs making these complex substances might introduce poisons by mistake.

LEGAL HIGHS

There are three common legal non-medical drugs. None of these drugs are harmless, but they are permitted, despite the risks, because they've been used for centuries.

Caffeine, in coffee and other drinks, is a stimulant that increases alertness. Too much prevents people sleeping well, which leads to health problems.

Alcohol is mostly a depressant, meaning it slows down body processes. In small amounts, it can be enjoyable. Large quantities result in physical illness and mental and social problems.

Nicotine, the drug in tobacco, works as both a depressant and a stimulant, and is highly addictive. The chemicals in the cigarette smoke cause cancers and lung diseases.

Illegal drugs such as cocaine (a powerful stimulant) and heroin (a painkiller and depressant) are banned because they are extremely addictive and carry a high risk of overdose, which can cause serious health problems, or even death. They also create a very big change in the way you feel, so big that it will block out other aspects of your feelings, both good and bad. It is never a good idea to use illegal drugs to block out your true feelings. It will just make bad things much worse.

WHAT'S WHAT?

HALLUCINOGENS

Cannabis and some other drugs are hallucinogens – they make you see and hear things that are not there. Psychologists have discovered that much of our perception of the world around us is a mental model of our surroundings rather than a real-time playback of information coming from the senses. However, sense information is used to update our mental picture of what is going on. Hallucinogens interfere with this system.

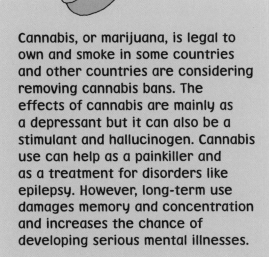

Cannabis, or marijuana, is legal to own and smoke in some countries and other countries are considering removing cannabis bans. The effects of cannabis are mainly as a depressant but it can also be a stimulant and hallucinogen. Cannabis use can help as a painkiller and as a treatment for disorders like epilepsy. However, long-term use damages memory and concentration and increases the chance of developing serious mental illnesses.

SMART DRUGS

Some drugs make your memory better, help you focus on tasks, generate ideas and make decisions quickly. The technical term for them is nootropic or cognitive enhancer. Maybe in the future it will be normal to take nootropics for school tests or job interviews. We sort of use them already. Caffeine is a nootropic, which is one reason people drink it when they are busy.

BODYBUILDING DRUGS

Anabolic steroids are drugs that mimic the natural chemicals used by humans to grow muscles, so taking these drugs makes the body build muscles more quickly during training. These powerful drugs can do great harm if misused; damage to the heart is a common side-effect. Sports people using steroids are seen as cheats, but the same drugs are being tested for use by soldiers. If the side-effects can be managed, elite forces may use steroids to be bigger and tougher than their enemies.

Antidepressant drugs work by helping to stop unpleasant thoughts, which add up to create feelings of dread, sadness or anxiety. The most common type are called SSRIs, which stands for selective serotonin re-uptake inhibitor. Very simply, they stop the brain reducing the levels of serotonin, a brain chemical associated with a good mood. In Western countries, between 5 and 10 per cent of people take an SSRI drug.

BRAVE NEW WORLD

In 1932, British author Aldous Huxley wrote a book called *Brave New World*, which imagines a future society where people are made, not born. Everyone in the story takes a drug called 'soma'. It works like alcohol, cannabis, a cognitive enhancer and an antidepressant rolled into one. Soma makes everyone happy and content, but in return they have to give up control over their lives. Does that sound like a good thing?

Militaries throughout history have used drugs, whether officially or unofficially, to alter the mental and physical states of soldiers for combat. These usually include drugs to keep soldiers awake and alert for two or three days at a time. They are effective but usually come with extreme side effects. Do the benefits outweigh the risks?

WHAT'S WHAT?

TRUTH SERUMS

In the 20th century, a lot of attention was given to finding a drug that made it impossible for a person to tell a lie. Several chemicals seemed to have some effect. However, it was later found that the drugs also made people very suggestible, and they were very likely to be making things up so they could agree with whatever their questioner was saying. So in the end, truth serums often made people even bigger liars.

ARE DRUGS A SOLUTION?

Using chemicals to change the way the body and mind are working has risks and rewards. If the risks can be minimised, will taking drugs to make us happy and healthy become a normal activity in the future? If everyone could take a pill to make them happy, what would happen to those who refused?

GENETIC MODIFICATION

Genetic engineers first worked out how to edit genes in the 1970s. At first, they made genetically modified microbes and created new disease-resistant crops. Today's GMOs (genetically modified organisms) include mice that glow in the dark and goats that produce spider's silk in their milk. However, the use of genetic engineering on humans has been very heavily controlled. As the technology gets easier to use, will we start to genetically modify ourselves? What genes would you like added?

CRISPR

The gene-editing system, CRISPR (pronounced 'crisper'), was developed in 2012. It makes use of the defence system inside a bacteria that slices up the DNA of an attacking virus. (A virus is a piece of DNA that hijacks a cell. DNA is the chemical that carries genes.) The CRISPR system's slicing abilities can be used to cut any DNA at a very precise place and then a new bit of DNA can be added.

CRISPR is used to modify simple organisms such as bacteria or yeast. Genes from other lifeforms (or ones designed) are added to make the bug do a particular job. The results are synthetic organisms, and they may prove very useful. We already use GM bacteria to make medicines. Scientists are now trying to engineer algae that make fuel from sunlight instead of sugars, and bacteria that eat plastic or other waste.

Early genetic engineering systems would not work on humans. The new DNA was wound around specks of gold dust and blasted at target cells with a device called a 'gene gun'. Most of the cells just got splatted, while every now and then, a grain of gold and its DNA cargo got into the cell without killing it. This success rate would be much too low to be useful in medicine, but the knowledge gained by scientists paved the way to future developments.

WHAT'S WHAT?

A GENE

The word 'gene' is tricky to define. A gene is a piece of DNA (deoxyribonucleic acid) that carries the code for making one protein used to build a body. But a gene is also a characteristic that can be inherited, like hair and skin colour or face shape. Genetics is the science that tries to work out how the first idea of a gene relates to the second one.

PASSING IT ON

There are two ways of modifying an organism's genes. Genes can be added to the body to fix a problem caused by a gene that is present naturally. This is a one-time change which won't be passed to the next generation. The second method is to change the genes in the organism's germline, the cells that produce the sperm or eggs that combine to make the next generation. Germline modification changes the genes passed on from generation to generation forever.

BIOHACKERS

'Biohackers' have tried to use CRISPR tech to change their own genes, injecting themselves with genes to make their muscles grow or change their skin colour. It is risky in many ways, and it doesn't work. CRISPR can edit a single-celled creature like a germ, it has little effect on the human body's 30 trillion cells. To have an effect on a human you would need to edit the germline, and that is illegal (at the moment).

Most of a baby's genes come equally from each parent, but a tiny quantity of DNA comes only from the mother. This is part of the mitochondria, the power sources inside each cell. Damaged mitochondria means a baby will have a very serious disease. Since 2018 doctors have been allowed to replace damaged mitochondria from the mother's egg with healthy ones from another woman. Then the father's sperm is used to fertilize the egg, making a disease-free GM baby with three parents. This technique can save lives but it also makes it possible to alter other genes in the baby. Is that progress?

DESIGNER BABIES

Editing the human germline would allow parents to design their children. What would you choose? High intelligence, good looks, a strong body and perfect health, obviously. Would you want them to look like you – or your favourite TV star? You could add in genes from other organisms. Imagine kids that glow in the dark like a jellyfish, or have animal abilities like ultrasonic hearing from bats, electro-detection from a shark or heat sensors from a snake!

FIGHTING DISEASE

Some rare genes give immunity to dangerous diseases. Adding these genes to the next generation seems like a good idea and it's easy enough to do – one person at a time. Only the wealthiest could afford such genetic modification. People who couldn't afford it might become second-class citizens, left to the mercy of the disease. So even with this simple example of disease control, we need to consider the impact of genetic modification on society before we allow it to happen.

In 2003, the entire human genome was decoded. The genome is the genetic code carried in every human cell. Every human carries the same set of genes for building a body, but the instructions are all slightly different, making each person unique. We know humans have about 22,300 genes, but we don't yet know what each bit of DNA does and how variations affect the body and mind. We need to know a lot more before we can design a human safely.

WHO'S WHO?

HE JIANKUI

In 2019, this Chinese geneticist announced that he had edited the genes of twin girls using CRISPR. He changed the gene that controls immune cells, which he said would give the girls immunity to HIV infection. Since then, he has been under house arrest while the authorities investigate his claims. The danger is that He's edits will create health problems in the girls, but it could take years to find out.

STEM CELL THERAPY

Every body cell is specialised to do one job – for example, to be a blood cell or a bone cell. All cells have the same genetic instructions, but unneeded genes are switched off. Stem cells have the power to transform into any kind of cell. The main form of gene therapy replaces faulty body cells with modified stem cells. However, adult bodies stop making the most powerful kind of stem cells, so geneticists are learning how to switch the genes of specialised cells back on.

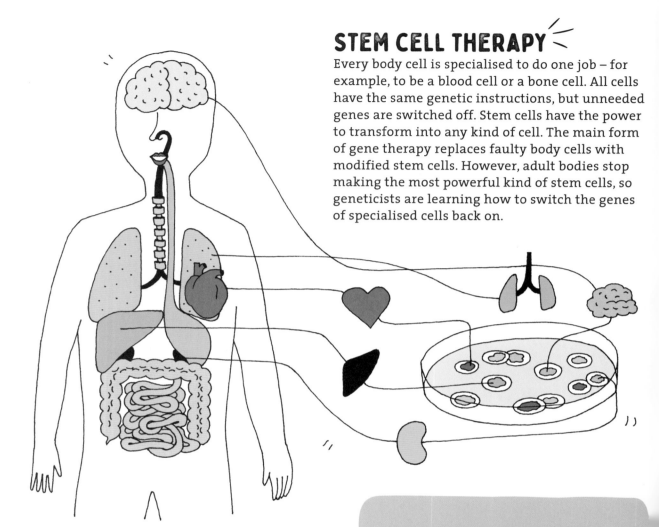

GENE THERAPY

The gene-editing tech that might be used for designer babies is already being developed to save lives. Gene therapy seeks to modify genes in a faulty body part. As these changes fix the problem but are not passed to the next generation, gene therapy is legal. Genes are usually introduced into the target cells using a genetically modified virus. Gene therapy uses viruses that do not cause illness, and they are modified to 'infect' only the correct cells.

Stem cells are found in places like bone marrow and fat. These cells can only transform into a small set of tissues, such as bone and muscle. Scientists are working out how to make them grow into a wider range of cells, such as nerve cells. The most powerful stem cells, called totipotent stem cells, are found in an embryo, the tiny ball of cells just starting to grow into a body. We'll look at how these cells could be used, and whether they should be, later in the book.

GENETIC MEDICINE

The more we understand about how human genes work, the better able doctors will be to develop treatments designed according to each patient's genetic make-up. An example of genetic medicine is gene silencing, which uses a drug that is designed to attack a precise strand of faulty DNA, preventing it from sending its coded instructions out to the cell. Gene-silencing drugs are likely to become a common therapy for incurable genetic disorders in the near future.

WHAT'S WHAT?

EPIGENETICS

Epigenetics is more interested in the chemicals on the chromosomes than the DNA itself. These chemicals, called the epigenome, change according to how fit and healthy you are, and which genes your body needs to use. You pass your epigenome on to your kids and even grandkids! It is early days, but it appears that the epigenome might be an important part of fully understanding how we inherit certain characteristics.

DNA is delicate stuff. There are 2 metres of it in each of your cells, coiled up on 46 holders called 'chromosomes', which are about two millionths of a metre long. Artificial DNA – XNA, or xeno nucleic acid – has been made much tougher. It can withstand chemicals and radiation that might damage DNA. Genetic engineers are trying to build living cells that use XNA. Perhaps future genetic modifications will involve replacing our body cells with tough XNA versions.

SHOULD WE 'DESIGN' BABIES?

If you had a choice between a healthy natural baby or a genetically designed one, which one would you choose? If many of the other children being born were designed, would that change your view?

CLONES

If you had a clone of yourself, what would you do with it? A clone is a genetic copy of you, with exactly the same set of genes. So a clone is like having an identical twin, only younger than you. The technology to make animal clones has existed for many years, but cloning a human is against the law. What would it take for that law to change in the future? Let's find out.

Dolly the sheep died in 2003. However, she lived on as four more clones called Daisy, Debbie, Dianna and Denise. If we could do it for Dolly, why don't we make copies of humans? The main reason is safety. Researchers tried 277 times to clone a sheep. Dolly was the first to survive. Some of the others developed horrible problems and the vets killed them to prevent suffering. Is it right for a doctor to do that with a human clone? Is it simply morally wrong to clone humans?

DOLLY THE SHEEP

The most famous clone was a sheep called Dolly, born in Scotland in 1996. She had three mothers and no father. Mother 1 provided a body cell from which the nucleus, where all the chromosomes are stored, was removed. An egg was taken from Mother 2. This had all its genes removed, and the nucleus from Mother 1 was inserted. The egg was given an electric shock, which made it begin growing into a baby sheep. Baby Dolly was put inside Mother 3, where she developed and was born normally.

STEM CELL SUPPLY

Animals (including sheep and humans) develop from a single cell called a zygote, which grows into a ball of cells. The cells are stem cells, which can develop into any kind of body cell. They have the same genes as your body cells, so a clone of you could form a supply of stem cells that could be harvested and used to fix all kinds of currently incurable problems. With a supply of cloned stem cells, you could just keep growing new hearts, lungs and other body bits.

WHAT'S WHAT?

PHARMING

Using genetically modified organisms to create medicines is called 'pharming' – a mash-up of pharmaceuticals and farming. Genetic tech might make it possible to make transgenic farm animals that have some human genes, specifically the genes that the body uses as an identity card for telling itself apart from invading bugs. Organs from a transgenic animal could then be transplanted into a human with less risk of rejection.

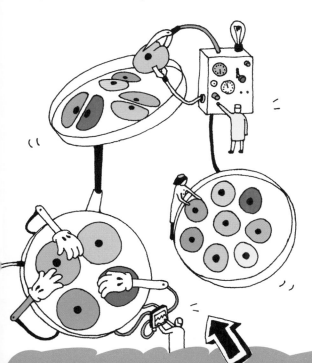

CLONE ARMY ANYONE?

In sci fi, cloning is sometimes done by a machine that works like an ultra high-tech photocopier. This would be a good way of building an army or labour force, but this isn't the way clones will work in the future. Our genes are important in shaping us but so is the environment we grow up in – things like our diet and the experiences we have. So despite their identical genes, even clones are unique individuals.

WHAT COUNTS AS A HUMAN BEING?

In the first five days of human development, it's impossible to tell which cells will grow into a baby and which will die away. On day six, the first cells in the human embryo are formed. Is this when a clone would become a human being? Or was it a human all along?

AGEING AND DEATH

In the last few decades, doctors have got better at keeping us alive for longer. However, as we get older our bodies are less able to stay healthy, so older people may spend many years living with illnesses. The way to prevent this is to stop the body from ageing in the first place. We can't make people younger, but we might be able to prevent the changes that happen to the body as it grows older.

SENESCENCE

Ageing is an active process called senescence. Even as you grew from a ball of cells, most of those cells were destroyed in the process of making new ones that became your body tissue. This balance of life and death continues until about the age of 30. Then more cells start dying than are renewed. This is what makes the body age. If doctors can work out how to slow – or stop – the process of senescence, that could mean we live longer, healthier lives.

Senescence is not the only ageing process. Depending on how unlucky or cautious you are, your body will pick up injuries and illnesses from time to time. Generally it can recover fully from this damage, but sometimes scars and other permanent weaknesses can't be avoided, which might increase the impact of senescence in later life.

MENOPAUSE

Most species are able to reproduce for their whole lives. Humans, along with a few kinds of whale, have a menopause, where the female reproductive system turns off. So why do women outlive their fertility? This is something that has long puzzled evolutionary biologists. One popular theory is the 'grandmother hypothesis' which argues that post-menopausal females who are no longer sexually competitive could focus on passing on their wisdom and care for the youngsters.

TWO KINDS OF DEATH

There are only two ways to die:
Cardiac death: The heart might stop if it fails, or even if another part of the body has failed. If doctors can fix the heart or the other problem, they may be able to restart the heart and bring the body back from the brink of death.
Brain death: The heart is controlled by the brain stem, which works on autopilot, but if the rest of the brain – and the mind – has ceased to function, then we generally agree that death has occurred, even if the heart is still pumping. It takes some time to confirm. Doctors usually add radioactive markers to the blood supply to check. If none of the markers end up in the brain, brain death is proved.

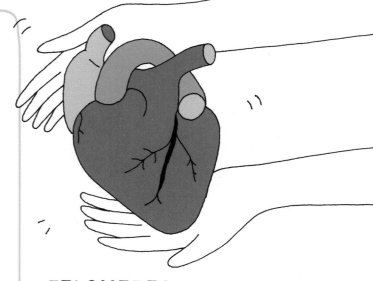

TELOMERES

The key to ageing is in genes. Particular genes give some people healthy, youthful bodies, even in old age. Scientists are trying to understand these genes better by studying telomeres. These are found on the ends of chromosomes and work like molecular counters. Every time a chromosome is copied, just before a cell divides into two, a telomere drops off. Once the chromosome runs out of telomeres, it can't divide again, and the cell will die. Learning to control this system will be a key to creating anti-ageing medicine.

CRYONICS

The best way to try to stay young is to lead a healthy life – be active and eat plenty of fresh nuts, grains and green veg. However, the time will come when the body cannot support life anymore. Some people have opted to be preserved after death, their bodies frozen in liquid nitrogen. The idea of the process, called cryonics, is that eventually technology will be able to revive them – and presumably fix whatever killed them in the first place.

REVERSING DEATH

When the body dies, the systems that keep it going have failed to work together. The cells stay intact for several hours, and, if treated correctly, can be preserved for much longer. Problems arise when doctors try to revive the cells by supplying them with oxygen and nutrients, which often kills the cells. However, in 2019 researchers announced that they had been able to revive dead pig brains, at least a bit. Maybe it really will be possible to reverse death in the future.

Cryonics was developed in the late 1960s by the American Robert Ettinger. He set up an organisation called the Immortalist Society to run the process after his death. When Robert died in 2003, he was immediately preserved. Although he's already dead, switching off his freezer seems very wrong because it would meaning killing his possible future self. So in some ways Robert is already immortal (just not in a very exciting way).

ETERNAL RISKS

What would it be like to live forever? Let's assume the problems of ageing and disease are solved. You are healthy and strong, but you can still be killed by some violent accident. What would your world be like? Would you cross the road? Obviously if you are careful, the chances of being run over are low. But if you lived forever, you will almost certainly get hit by a car at some point!

WHO'S WHO?

TITHONUS

The Greek goddess of dawn, Eos, fell in love with a mortal human, Tithonus. She asked the king of the gods, Zeus, to make her boyfriend immortal. Zeus agreed but still punished the pair for their request. Tithonus would never die but he still got older and more decrepit. Eventually he turned into a cicada that could do nothing but chirp.

WHAT'S WHAT?

ELIXIR OF LIFE

For centuries people believed in the philosopher's stone, a magical substance that could turn lead into gold. Wizard-like researchers called alchemists tried to work out how to make it. Even Isaac Newton had a go. Alchemists also searched for the elixir of life, a drink that made you live forever, and the panacea, a cure for all diseases. We may have given up on the philosopher's stone, but we still hold out hope for the other two.

DO YOU WANT TO LIVE FOREVER?

If you never grew old, what would you do with your time? Would it make a difference if you were the only immortal person, always meeting new people? Or would you want everyone to be immortal?

NANOTECHNOLOGY

Imagine a machine so small it could be injected into your body. This is nanotechnology, where devices are measured in nanometres – that's billionths of a metre. Such a machine – let's call it a 'nanobot' – would be around the size of a virus, and it could travel around the body in the blood and go in and out of cells. It might sound like science fiction, but nanotechnology is already a real thing – we'll have to wait for nanobots, though.

NANOBOTS

Nanobots will look a lot more like atomic caterpillars or molecular egg whisks than miniature androids. Nanoengineers take their inspiration for designs of experimental nanobots – the experts call them nanites – from complex molecules in our cells, such as proteins and DNA. These are large molecules made by stringing together smaller ones called monomers. By assembling the right monomers in a very specific order, nanoengineers have made nanoscale switches, propellers, tweezers and even a nanocar that rolls on four wheels.

NANOMEDICINE

Nanomachines could carry powerful drugs into the body, perhaps inside a cage of atoms to prevent it attacking healthy body parts. The machine would be programmed to have a padlock which is only openable by the unique chemical tags on the drug's target, such as a cancer or virus. Also nanobots might work like construction workers to assemble sections of nanotubes (made from rolled-up graphene) into long pipes to repair severed nerves or damaged blood vessels.

Of course, anything can be measured in nanometres (nm). The Titanic was 269 billion nanometres long but that does not make it a nanobot. Things made to be between 10 and 100 nanometres are counted as nanotechnology. A bacterial cell is far larger, at 1,000 nm. Making a nanobot smaller than 10 nm is unlikely because this is getting down to the size of chemical molecules like sugar and fat and there would not be enough atoms to build machines with.

WHAT'S WHAT?

GRAPHENE

A lot of nanotechnology will use a form of pure carbon called graphene. Graphene atoms are arranged in interconnecting hexagons that make a sheet just one atom thick. Graphene is super strong, it conducts electricity and it can be formed into tubes and balls. The future could be made from graphene.

GECKO FEET

Geckos' feet can stick to any surface, enabling these lizards to walk on the ceiling as easily as the ground. The stickiness comes from billions of nanoscale hairs that each grip a little and, together, they grip a lot. A nanotechnology called 'gecko tape' uses nanotubes to copy this system. Gecko tape shoes and gloves – or even a coating on the skin – might allow you to climb walls like a gecko (or Spider-man, take your pick).

Nanotechnology is already used in some unlikely places. Sunscreen blocks out dangerous rays using nanoscale particles of zinc or titanium oxide. Scratch-resistant glass is toughened with a layer of nanoscopic aluminium-rich powders, which make a rock-hard coating. The Romans used gold nanoparticles in their finest glassware (without realizing they were being nanotechnicians). When light shines through the glass from behind, it looks red, but light from the front makes it green!

WOULD YOU WANT NANOBOTS IN YOU?

How do you feel about nanotechnology working inside your body? Is it okay so long as they help you? Would you worry that they could be put there without your knowledge or permission?

BIOPRINTING

The invention of the printing press was one of the most significant in human history. After all, it made this book possible. Just as society is becoming more paperless, printing has been reinvented to build 3D objects. 3D-printing technology was developed to use blobs of plastic, but it works the same with any gloopy liquid — even the cells of the human body. Could it be that one day we will be able to print body parts? Let's find out.

THE PRINTING PROCESS

Inkjet printers, like you might have at home, squirt out tiny blobs of ink which dry into a pattern of dots to create text and pictures. If you change the ink to warm, gooey plastic, instead of a dot you get a small blob of solid plastic that you can build up layer upon layer to construct all kinds of shapes. Replace the plastic with bio-ink – a mixture of body cells and jelly substances to bond the cells – and you can construct living tissue.

ORGAN ON A CHIP

One of the areas of bioprinting that is already well developed is the idea of printing several different tissue layers and connecting them to make an organ system in miniature. Known as 'organs-on-a-chip', these structures are not meant to be replacement body parts. Instead, they are a quick and easy way to study the organ, for example for testing it with drugs and poisons or working out how it develops cancers.

There's a lot of work still to be done, but eventually it could take just a few days to create new body parts ready to transplant. It isn't quite as simple as pressing 'print'. The 'bioprint' design must include nerves, blood vessels and other connections to the rest of the body. This can be done by copying a 3D scan of a real body part. After bioprinting, the structure must be brought to life by supplying it with nutrients, chemical messengers and nerve signals.

Another approach to bioprinting is to use the cells' own ability to grow into a particular organ or body part. Cells grow by sending signals to each other. Self-assembling bioprints would hack these signals to tell the cells in the bio-ink (or another source of cells) to arrange themselves in a certain way.

MAGNETIC BIOPRINTING

Bio-inks have been merged with nanotechnology. Tiny fragments of magnetic iron are added to the cells in the bio-ink. Instead of being squirted out into patterns, the bio-ink is then arranged using a magnetic field. This is similar to the way a laser printer or photocopier works. Magnetic bio-printing could be a way of speeding up the process.

WHAT'S WHAT?

PRINTED FOOD

The techniques used to print body parts can be used to create food. In fact, it is much easier because food does not need to be brought to life after being printed. In the future the meat we eat might be made like this. Livestock farming is more damaging to the environment than growing plants, so it might prove less polluting to make muscle cells in a factory and print them out as burgers, chops and steaks. Yum?

SHOULD WE ALL BE 'BODY BUILDERS'?

Should people be allowed to have their own bioprinters at home? Would it be OK for them to create any body parts they want? Or should changes like these always be controlled by experts?

Forget improving the body using its own biology – let's go bionic! Bionics are mechanical body parts that replace and improve on the natural version. In the future, we may add bionic enhancements to our bodies, and that would make us cyborgs (short for cybernetic organisms). Some people already have bionic legs, arms and electrical implants in their bodies. Cyborg technology could go much further, transforming people into half-human, half-robot. Let's look at why we might want to do that.

EXOSKELETON

Exoskeletons are devices worn outside the body that take over – or add to – its movements. This kind of tech is being developed to help paralysed people walk again. Military versions will allow soldiers to carry heavier packs and march faster for longer. Breakthroughs in exoskeleton technology depend on getting the power-to-weight ratio correct. A powerful suit would be heavy and difficult to use, while a lightweight one would be less strong and would soon run out of power.

Exoskeletons might not be robotic levers and motors attached to arms and legs. They could be a skin-tight body suit made from fabric that works like muscles, getting shorter and pulling on the skeleton. Top contenders for making artificial muscle fabric include plastics that twitch when electrified. Muscles could also be made from bundles of spider silk which shrinks when wet, expands when dry and is stronger than steel.

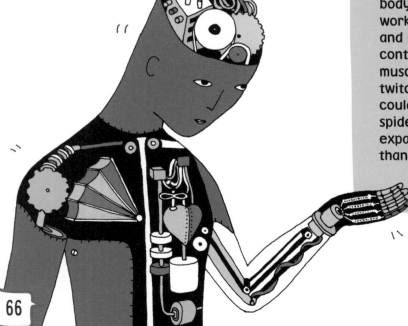

JET MAN

Cyborgs are not limited to two arms and two legs. Why not add some wings? That's what Yves Rossy, A.K.A Jet Man, has done. He has designed a wing he can wear. Powered by four tiny jet engines, each weighing just 3.5 kilograms, it gives him a top speed of 300 kilometres per hour.

TELEPRESENCE

Why bother converting your body into a robot when you can live as a robot temporarily. 'Telepresence' combines basic videoconferencing systems with a simple robot on wheels. The robot's face is a screen, through which you can see people and they can see you – you get the picture. You can navigate your robot around an office or house so you can attend meetings or visit friends, almost as if you were in the room with them.

AUGMENTED REALITY (AR)

Also known as mixed reality, this is one of the core skills of cyborgs. Human senses are combined with information from elsewhere via sensors on the body or through connections with other cyborgs or the Internet. The AR will relay information in the form of text and pictures in their vision or as additional sounds, or it may use the other senses. Perhaps AR could create a bad smell when the air is polluted or a sample taste of items on a takeaway menu.

You might already have a mixed reality device, such as a fitness tracker or a smart watch. Other wearables include smart spectacles that work like screens in front of the eye. Contact lenses are being developed to do the same thing. The big hurdle here is power supply. How do you make a battery powerful enough to run the device but small enough to fit into your eye? The solution might be smart clothing that harvests energy from movements to power wearable devices wirelessly.

EXTENDING VISION

Light is electromagnetic (EM) radiation that our eyes can detect, but there is a whole spectrum of EM radiation that is invisible to humans. A cyborg vision system would use digital camera technology to see invisible light, such as infrared and ultraviolet. The simplest method might be to replace natural eyes at birth, so a baby's brain can teach itself to make images from the signals coming from the cyborg eye.

ENHANCED HEARING

Sometimes, people have trouble hearing because sounds cannot reach the inner ear, or cochlea, where they are converted into nerve signals for the brain. A cochlear implant connects a microphone on the outside of the head to the cochlea through a hole drilled in the skull. A cyborg could use this implant to enhance their hearing. The microphone could pick up deep sounds coming from the ocean or high-pitched ultrasounds used by bats and dolphins.

Colour is your brain's way of showing the wavelength of light beams. Three kinds of cone cell in the back of the eye detect three distinct bands of wavelengths, which we see as red, green and blue (or mixtures of all three). Imagine what it would look like if a brain received five or more colour types, including the infrared and ultraviolet wavelengths.

BLOCKING SENSES

It might be annoying to have these cyborg super-senses all the time, but unlike our natural senses, cyborg senses could be set up to block out the sights, sounds, smells or tastes that you don't like. In a cyborg future, avoiding people you fall out with could go to a whole new level – you would never have to see them again, even if they were standing in front of you. Would that be good for friendships and society?

Surgeons often have to use their sense of touch to feel around inside the body without a good view. It must be very hard to feel your way through those slippery innards. A cyborg system has been developed to help. Surgeons wear electronic pads on their fingertips. These create a tingling sensation when they touch some slimy guts, enhancing the surgeons' sense of touch.

NEIL HARBISSON

Born with a rare kind of colour-blindness, Neil Harbisson only sees in black and white. In 2004, when he was 20, he had an antenna screwed into his skull which can detect EM radiation, including coloured light, infrared, ultraviolet and radio signals. It vibrates when it picks up radiation, so Harbisson can feel and hear different colours. Along with a fellow cyborg, Moon Ribas, Harbisson has had a 'bluetooth tooth' installed. Biting on one tooth makes the other person's buzz, allowing the two to exchange coded messages.

SILENT SPEECH

A big step in building a cyborg is to make a computer connection with the brain. In 2019, scientists in San Francisco tapped into the nerves that control the tongue and larynx used for speaking. Thinking about speaking sends signals down these nerves so a computer can use these signals to work out what the person intends to say. The system has been designed so people who cannot speak can use a simulated voice. Just imagine what else it might be used for.

Telepathy - sending messages using the power of thought - is impossible between human minds, but a cyborg is more than human. As a cyborg with silent speech technology, you could send and receive messages just by thinking them. The message might appear in your AR screen or digital eye, or your enhanced hearing system could convert the message into a voice that only you can hear. It might get quite noisy inside your head.

Brain interface systems based on brain waves are being developed to give people control over prosthetic limbs and other implants. It takes a lot of practice to train the brain to think in the right way, but it could become an almost unconscious skill. If the system can be perfected it could be used to remotely control devices like drones or to give a cyborg the power of telekinesis – the ability to move objects just by using thoughts.

HACKING THE MIND'S EYE

Light detected by the eyes is converted into a pattern of electrical signals in a layer of cells at the back of the brain. Researchers are looking at ways to record these patterns and so record what people are seeing. The same vision system is used when people imagine images in their mind's eye. If the system can be cracked, then a cyborg could send and receive imagined images and even record their dreams as they slept.

EXOMEMORY

Does the human memory get full? We certainly forget things, through age or laziness, or as old memories are deleted to make way for new ones. A cyborg will be able to simply connect to the World Wide Web and have all their information appear in their mind. The data on the web will serve as the cyborg's 'exomemory', or external memory. In many respects our devices allow us to work like this already.

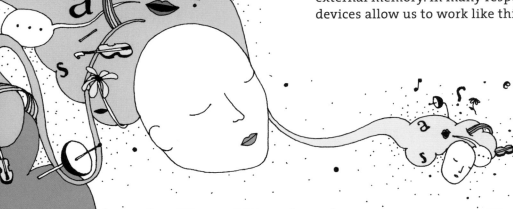

SHOULD WE LET OTHERS READ OUR MINDS?

Would the convenience of giving technology access to your thoughts be worth the risk of someone hacking into it? The technology could also make it impossible to keep secrets. What would a world be like without secrets?

UPLOADING

Human consciousness is created in the brain. When the body fails, the brain fails too and consciousness fades away. Efforts to repair the body, slow ageing or replace our biology with cyborg machinery are all efforts to maintain consciousness. A future technology called 'mind uploading' might make all that unnecessary. We could transfer a consciousness to a computer, where it could exist forever. Some say it's impossible; others say we'll be doing it before 2050. Who's correct?

COMPUTING POWER

To make a computer model of the brain's electrical activity would require a supercomputer that can do 10 billion trillion calculations per second and has a trillion terabytes of memory (about the same as a trillion laptop computers). In addition, to emulate the chemical reactions taking place in every brain cell would require 100 trillion trillion trillion times more memory. A computer that can do all that needs to do 10 million trillion trillion trillion calculations per second. Today's fastest computer can only do 33,000 trillion per second!

HOW COULD IT WORK?

Where do you begin with uploading an entire mind? It's not as simple as transferring memories into a database, like backing up your photos. To make a copy of a mind, a computer emulation of the entire human brain will be needed. The computer would need a processing system to link memories and merge them with signals from the senses – digital versions of the eyes, ears, nose and so on. Will that be enough to recreate your consciousness?

ARE YOU THERE?

So let's imagine a computer has been created that can simulate every aspect of a brain. Is this simulation of your brain really you? The software outputs an interaction with the real world – it could be a face on a screen or it could be an android, a human-like robot, that looks just like you. If your mind did copy over successfully, how could you convince the humans that it did? Will anyone believe that it is you in there? Would you?

STARCHIP

Mind uploading might be the only way we travel to the stars. 'StarChips' are tiny starships. StarChips could reach speeds of a third of the speed of light and travel to nearby stars in 20 years. That's too long for a biological crew, but a mind uploaded to the StarChip could be powered down for the journey and then booted up on arrival.

It is estimated that a supercomputer capable of simulating all the chemical reactions in a brain will take another hundred years to create – and to be cheap enough to build (costing only $1 million). Once your mind is hosted by this device, are you owned by whoever owns the computer? If you bought the computer before your body died, who owns it, and therefore you, now you're 'dead'? How does it work?

DO WE HAVE A RIGHT TO AN AFTERLIFE?

If a person's mind is uploaded when their body dies, does that mind have the same rights as a living human? Are we allowed to turn it off?

73

ROBOTICS

In the future, humans might not bother with their bodies at all. Instead they could be minds hosted by computers of immense power. An uploaded digital mind might choose to take control of a body. That body will be a robot. What shape will it be? The idea of a robot is ancient and has been thought up many times over around the world. Each time, people imagine a human-shaped machine that works as our slave. Is this the best kind of robot we can think of?

Robot designers are experts in biomimicry or copying the bodies of animals to build better robots. There are worm-bots, snake-bots, kangaroo-bots, fish-bots and robot jellyfish. No animal has ever evolved to use wheels, but wheels are faster than legs over flat surfaces, so the best robot design merges legs with wheels. One such device is BionicWheelBot, which can scuttle like a spider up and over walls, then curve its legs into a pair of wheels to roll away.

HOW TO BUILD A ROBOT

The word 'robot' is the Czech word for 'slave'. It was thought up in 1921 by Czech playwright Karel Capek in a tale of artificial humans who work as servants. Capek's idea spread, and people imagined mechanical humans with motors, pistons and levers – and that's how robots are built today. However, Capek's robots were made from the same materials as human bodies. Skin, bones and muscle are stronger and lighter than metal and plastic parts. In the future, robots might be built using cloning and bioprinting.

ANDROIDS AND ACTROIDS

Androids (robot people) could join human society, either controlled by an uploaded mind or by an artificial intelligence. It has even been suggested that these robot people should be called 'Robo sapiens' to distinguish them from *Homo sapiens*. If androids are to be accepted as people, they will need to look – and act – like us. One arm of robot research is to create 'actroids', robots with natural-looking soft rubber faces that can make facial expressions.

LAWS OF ROBOTICS

You may have heard that robots are going to take over and wipe out humans. However, sci-fi author Isaac Asimov imagined a world where robots were programmed with three simple rules, which ensured that humans would always be in charge:

First Law: A robot may not injure a human being or, through inaction, allow a human being to come to harm.

Second Law: A robot must obey the orders given it by human beings except where such orders would conflict with the First Law.

Third Law: A robot must protect its own existence as long as such protection does not conflict with the First or Second Laws.

WHAT'S WHAT?

THE UNCANNY VALLEY

The closer engineers manage to make androids look like living humans, the more strange and unsettling they appear to us. This feeling is called the 'uncanny valley'. We like the look of living people, and we like the way metal robots look too, but machines that look too human frighten us. It could be that actroids with their blank expressions and faces that don't move quite right, look a bit too much like dead people, and that scares us.

1ˢᵗ LAW

2ᴺᴰ LAW

3ᴿᴰ LAW

? DOES A ROBOT KNOW IT'S A ROBOT?

Because we know so little about how our own human consciousness works and why we dream, how can we know if a robot is conscious or dreaming? Perhaps they are, just in a different way?

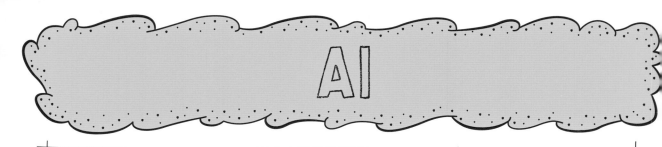

AI

AI stands for artificial intelligence. It is a type of software that can make decisions. Today, smart speakers use AI to work out what you said — that isn't always easy, but AI learns from its mistakes. AI makes suggestions for what to buy next at an online store and which video you might like on social media. Clever stuff! In the future, AI might become as clever as us — perhaps cleverer. Will that be good for us?

NARROW VS. GENERAL

The AI which is becoming common in everyday life is known as 'narrow AI'. It's good at detecting patterns, as in voice-recognition systems, or it can analyse data to calculate the chances of what happens next. Narrow AI can work faster, more accurately and for longer at this kind of job than a human. However, a narrow AI can't do anything else. A 'general AI' could know what it doesn't know and decide to learn new things. This is more like human intelligence. So far, general AI is beyond the scope of today's computer science.

EXPERT SYSTEMS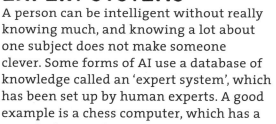

A person can be intelligent without really knowing much, and knowing a lot about one subject does not make someone clever. Some forms of AI use a database of knowledge called an 'expert system', which has been set up by human experts. A good example is a chess computer, which has a record of every chess game already played and so can always see the way to win a new game. In the future, human experts like doctors, lawyers and accountants might be replaced by AI expert systems.

MACHINE LEARNING

Artificial intelligence teaches itself by a process called 'machine learning'. Imagine an AI is tasked with recognising a cat in pictures. It analyses the data patterns of photos and sorts each picture into sets of 'cat' and 'no cat'. It is told what it got right and wrong and has another go. With each attempt, the AI works out the data patterns in a 'cat' picture. At the end of training, it can see a cat better than you can, and it can check millions of pictures every day.

Narrow AIs improve by collecting information from smart speakers, web searches and the like, and learning from it. However, some computer scientists worry that this type of machine learning will never produce a general AI as clever as you. To do that, they say, we need to crack the system our 83 trillion brain cells use to communicate. We know some are sent by electrical pulses, but have no way of decoding these signals. If we could work out 'brain code', we could build artificial brains to generate better AI.

Machine learning requires a type of computer processor called a 'neural network'. This system is inspired by the way the neurons (nerve cells) in the brain remember physical movements, like walking or playing the drums. Data inputs (such as a picture) travel a particular route through the layers that make up the neural network, resulting in an output: 'Cat!' The system learns by identifying which routes cat pictures take through the neural layers, as opposed to pictures without cats.

WHAT'S WHAT?

ALPHA GO

The cleverest AI around is AlphaGo, a programme for playing the board game Go. Go is simple to play, but there are more possible ways for one player to win than there are particles in the Universe, and no computer can work out all the options. Instead AlphaGo uses AI to beat its opponents with a mixture of machine learning, expert systems and advanced mathematics.

AUTONOMOUS MACHINES

Driverless cars use AI to decide how best to operate based on what they detect around themselves. That system isn't perfect yet, but if self-driving cars became the norm, they might have no owner. The car could earn money by giving people lifts, and that money would pay for fuel and repairs. The law would treat autonomous machines in a similar way to people. Does that mean a car would have the same rights as human?

THE TURING TEST

Named after computer science pioneer Alan Turing, this is one way of checking if a computer program is an AI. The Turing test sees a human judge hold a conversation with two hidden figures. One is human, the other is a 'chatbot', or computer that can talk or at least type replies. If the judge cannot tell which is the bot and which is the human, then the program is declared to be an AI. No program has ever passed, although some may have appeared to.

The big problem with the Turing test is summed up by an idea called the 'Chinese Room'. Imagine a chatbot is actually a man locked in a room. He speaks no Chinese but receives chat inputs in that language. He looks up the inputs in a book and copies out the answers – again in Chinese. His responses are perfect, but he doesn't understand them at all. The Turing test says this 'bot' is an AI, but the system has no understanding of what it is doing. Is that really intelligence?

WHO CONTROLS THE ALGORITHMS?

AIs program themselves, and so they write their own algorithms. In the future, AIs will manage the learning of other AI bots, and we'll allow these bots to control much more of our infrastructure – even our homes. Who's in control of all that AI? We cannot re-program it because we didn't program it in the first place. We'd have a choice: we either leave the AI on to do all the work, or turn it off and do the work instead.

WHAT'S WHAT?

EI

AI is generally judged by comparing it to human intelligence. However, there are other forms of natural intelligence or EI ('evolved intelligence'). Dolphins have large brains for processing information about sounds in the water. They may be able to see inside each other's bodies using ultrasound. Octopuses are another example of an EI that is different to ours. Their brain is distributed throughout the body, so they think as much with their arms as their heads.

An algorithm is a set of instructions arranged in a logical order that take an input and convert it into an output. Doing the washing up is an algorithm that converts dirty plates into clean ones. If you study it carefully, a good washing-up algorithm - where the plates do not break - is quite complex, but it is nothing like as complex as the ones used by AIs.

SHOULD THERE BE ARTIFICIAL RIGHTS?

Is it enough that an AI behaves like a human for it to have the same rights as a human? Even if it is thinking using a different system, does the act of thinking give it rights?

SUPERINTELLIGENCE

In 1965, Gordon Moore, a microchip engineer, predicted that chips (and the computers they controlled) would double in power every 18 months. This became known as 'Moore's Law', and so far it has been true. If this trend continues, computers will become cleverer than humans. A clever computer will eventually have an 'intelligence explosion'. It will write upgrades for itself over and over again until it becomes a superintelligence. Is this likely to happen?

Microchips are circuits of on-off switches called transistors, which can form a barrier that blocks an electric current. That barrier is getting narrower as transistors get smaller and microchips become more powerful. By around 2025, the barrier will only be a few atoms thick, and that will not be enough to block the current. The minimum size of silicon chips will have been reached, and Moore's Law will go into reverse: for computers to grow in power, they will need larger microchips.

BIG DATA

One explanation of human consciousness is that our brains are a system of systems which share information. Add enough information and the system becomes self-aware. The Internet is also a system of systems. In 1973, it connected around 100 computers; by 2023, it will connect 40 billion. Today's Internet also connects phones, cars and TVs in an 'Internet of Things'. This produces vast amounts of data – known as 'Big Data' – which AIs use in machine learning. Will an increasing amount of Big Data lead to the Internet becoming self-aware?

HOW WOULD WE KNOW?

Computer scientists call the moment that a computer starts to explode in intelligence the 'technological singularity'. How would we know it happened? Some experts joke that it already has. If you were a self-aware computer, how would you go about getting bigger and stronger? You could grow by adding more devices to your network. You could encourage people to feed your network with traffic. Videos of puppies, emojis – anything would do. Sound familiar? Maybe the Internet has reached 'singularity'. If it has, would we ever really know it?

QUANTUM COMPUTER

The limits of silicon-based computing make a superintelligence unlikely but a new system called quantum computing might be just the thing. Quantum computers have switches made from particles that obey the rules of quantum mechanics. That means they can be on and off at the same time. So 32 silicon-based computer switches hold 32 bits of information at a time (coded in 1s and 0s), but 32 quantum switches hold 4,294,967,29 bits. You can see how that might boost computer power.

COMMUNICATION WITH TECHNOLOGY

If a computer or network of computers becomes a superintelligence, will we be able to understand it? It might develop an awareness of itself that's as different to our intelligence as the mental processes of a dolphin or octopus. If anything, we should assume it can understand us – it is, after all, superintelligent – and maybe it will allow us to finally communicate with other lifeforms. I wonder what they will think about that?

IS IT FRIEND OR FOE?

Would a superintelligence want to enslave or destroy us? How could we defeat something so clever? A superintelligence might be able to solve many of the world's problems, but is it worth the risk?

IS THIS A SIMULATION?

When technology teams up with philosophy, the future becomes a very strange place — and so does the past. Let me explain. We've been imagining all the ways technology will change the world in this book. One possible outcome is that we discover our world is actually a program being run inside a computer of a future civilisation! So our past, present and future isn't real. It sounds crazy, but according to scientific logic, the 'Simulation Argument' is more likely to be true than false.

MATURE CIVILISATION

The Simulation Argument is the idea of Swedish philosopher Nick Bostrom. It relies on the idea of a mature civilisation that has an infinite computing power for simulating entire universes. There are technological hurdles to increasing computing power forever, such as the limits of silicon chips. Let's assume most civilisations fail to solve them, but a few do succeed. Of these, most fail to use the new technology safely and die out. Only a very few have the time and opportunities to develop full technological maturity. What do they do next?

WHY SIMULATE ANYWAY?

Why would a technologically mature civilisation bother to simulate universes? One reason is to model ancestors. We might all have lived these lives before, and our descendants might play them back to see what happened. Alternatively, our universe might be totally imaginary, made by an alien species as a game or as a pet that needs looking after. Finally, our universe might serve as a consciousness-processing unit of some far-future AI. Maybe.

The number of atoms in our universe is 10 with 80 zeroes after it, and there's about 3.5 cubic metres of space (about 20 bathtubs worth) for every single atom. A simulation would have to know the location of every atom plus hundreds of values for each one, such as its speed. When two atoms interact, their values change, and the effect of that interaction ripples out through space, changing the state of other particles. It gets complicated very quickly.

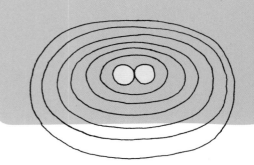

HOW TO FIND OUT

If just one mature society learns to simulate universes, they could create a huge number, and the chances are we are in one. So how do we find out? Simulations must set and follow rules, such as how hot and cold the universe can be. We know there is a minimum possible temperature (absolute zero, −273°C) but while we've theorised that there is a maximum temperature we haven't found an instant of it. So if we did find a maximum temperature (perhaps in an exploding star), that could prove that this really is a simulation.

WHAT'S WHAT?

A DYSON SPHERE

Mature civilisations need a lot of power. British physicist Freeman Dyson suggested the only way to get it is to build a vast solar power array around a star. The array – called a 'Dyson sphere' – would dim the star in such a way that other civilisations that understood the idea could recognise what was going on. So far, human astronomers haven't discovered any Dyson spheres.

IS IGNORANCE BLISS?

If you were a simulation, would you want to know? Perhaps it would be better to just never know and think this was all 'real'? However, even if this universe is a simulation, does that mean it can't also be real, or real enough?

POST-HUMAN SPECIES

There are around 9 million living species on Earth today. However, that represents just one per cent of all the species that have ever lived on the planet. All the others are extinct. I'm afraid to say that *Homo sapiens* will also join the ranks of the extinct at some point. The removal of one species offers an opportunity for another to take its place. Let's work through some possibilities for the post-human world.

WHERE WILL HUMANS GO?

Extinction can occur naturally over thousands of years, as one species forces another out. There are also mass extinctions, where many species die out at the same time. Scientists fear that humans are causing a mass extinction now. The extinction rate today is at least 1,000 times higher than it was 10,000 years ago, caused by climate change, habitat destruction, introduced species like cats and rats, and environmental pollutants. Might we humans be at risk of this extinction as well?

INSECT INVADERS

If humans became extinct there would be a big gap in the natural world for a species to evolve into an opportunistic omnivore. It is often said that cockroaches are so tough they will outlive humans. That may be true, but the really smart insects are ants. An ant colony is a kind of superorganism, a single living thing made up of thousands of individuals working together using a chemical communication system. If an ant superorganism gets big enough, might it develop awareness like our brain?

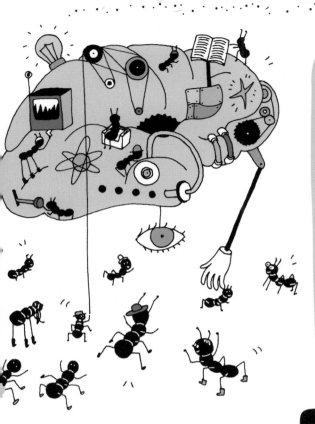

Humans are generalists, which means we can work out a way to survive in just about any habitat. Any species that takes over from us will need the same ability. One example of a generalist species that lives in all kinds of places is the raccoon. This naturally curious animal finds enough food by investigating every nook and cranny. The raccoon also has hand-like paws for holding food. Once humans have gone, it might be the raccoons that take over the world.

LIVING IN TEAMS

Our ancient human ancestors formed tight-knit bands who used language to get organised enough to survive. Today, animals that live like that include African meerkats, which take turns to stand guard and call warnings when danger approaches. The prairie dogs of North America (actually big squirrels) also live this way, and biologists think that their language skills are the most sophisticated in the animal kingdom after our own. Maybe that puts prairie dogs in the lead to replace us?

WHAT'S WHAT?

WOOD-WIDE WEB

Tree roots are connected to thin threads of fungi which help the tree collect nutrients from the soil and are rewarded with sugar from the tree. Trees and bushes of the same species are connected through the fungal network, which allows them to communicate in a kind of natural Internet which has been called the 'Wood-Wide Web'. This network sends nutrients to starving plants and spreads chemicals that stop other species invading the area. Is it really the plant kingdom – not us humans – that have developed the most advanced communication network?

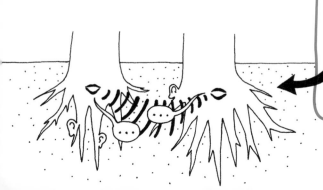

SPACE PEOPLE

In the nearly 60 years that humans have been going into space, we have found that living up there isn't easy. To begin with, it is common to feel sick for a few days. After several months, the lack of gravity weakens bones and muscles. A species of human that lived all its life in space would be too weak to visit Earth without a robotic exoskeleton to help them balance and walk.

PSEUDOEXTINCTION

Few biologists think that the human race will be a dead end for evolution. We are too clever to allow ourselves to become extinct, right? It's more likely that we will evolve into a range of post-human species. While there will be no more *Homo sapiens* left alive at some point, this will only be a pseudoextinction. Our descendants will survive as different species, depending on the new habitats they occupy, in space, on other worlds or beneath the planet's surface.

A post-human species might develop technology for producing babies without pregnancy or birth. Babies might be grown in – what shall we call it – a factory, a hive? If this were the case, why bother with having two sexes? Babies could be made asexually, using a mix of cloning and GM tech, and have no mother or father. What will this post-human species look like? A man or a woman, or something in between?

Climate change might force humans to spend long periods underground to avoid high temperatures on the surface. It is darker down there, so our eyesight might evolve to be black and white, which works better in faint light. It would also be humid in our subterranean lairs, so we would evolve thicker skin, and our sweat would be slimy to make a barrier that stops fungal infections.

WHO'S WHO?

MARTIANS

The most likely place for a new human species to appear is in a colony on Mars. Low gravity would mean bone and muscle grow slowly, making the whole body smaller and weaker. This will mean that only the toughest Martians survive, so the species could then evolve to be taller and stronger than us. Mars is almost always below freezing, so Martians might have long body hair to keep them warm.

WATER HUMANS

If a future human species were to adapt to life in water, we might expect them to have webbed hands and long, paddle-shaped feet. They would develop larger lungs for taking in air, and bigger spleens, which would work like a blood reservoir to store oxygen on long dives. Other aquatic animals take oxygen from the water through the soft lining of the mouth or anus. Perhaps our aquatic descendants will also evolve to breathe through their bums!

WHAT FUTURE WOULD YOU CHOOSE?

Which kind of posthuman would you like to be? Or would you prefer to stay just as you are? What do we need to do as a species to ensure our survival?

We've taken a close look at the human body and how it might change in the future. How do you feel about it? Are you excited by mind-uploading or immortality? Are you looking forward to designing yourself a new cyborg body or a baby with upgrades? Or are you terrified by the impact of genetic modification and AI? There's a lot to weigh up. It might help to think about the ways we can understand morality and ethics, the systems that we use to divide good from bad.

Utilitarianism is an ethics system that treats positive and negative consequences like a sum. It says that the idea of morality is to increase the positive consequences (happiness) and minimise negative ones (pain), and so every deed should be judged on its ability to do that. Taking this literally, however, we might find problems. Your happiness could be boosted a little by a gift of £10. Say the richest person in the world has £70 billion, enough to give everyone else £10. Would the pain caused by that person losing their money be outweighed by the happiness of 7 billion people getting free money?

CONSEQUENCES

'All's well that ends well', that is one way to judge whether you made the right decision. This way of thinking bases good and bad on the consequence of someone's actions. Imagine throwing a heavy stone over your head so it falls somewhere behind you. You do it 100 times and on just one occasion the stone hits someone and hurts them. Were all 100 of your actions bad, or just the harmful one?

Perhaps a better form of utilitarianism is summed up by the harm principle. Instead of having a very long list of behaviours that are agreed to be good, you can do whatever you like as long as it does not cause any harm to someone else. However, are you allowed to harm yourself? And is it ever possible to harm yourself without harming someone else at least a little?

WHAT'S WHAT?

RELATIVISM

According to this school of thought what we regard as good and bad changes as society develops and learns more about the world and how to control it in useful ways. And that means that a good behaviour is whatever you can get away with without the rest of society stopping you, either using laws or social condemnation. This means that what was a crime in the past may be allowed today, and what might be normal behaviour in one country is frowned upon in another.

VIRTUE

This is an old-fashioned way of understanding good and bad that dates back to the days of the ancient Greeks. It says that a good behaviour is one that shows off how you are a virtuous person with qualities such as generosity, kindness, and patience. Behaving badly is guided by bad personal qualities and leads to you being unhappy, and that is the reason not to do it. Virtue ethics can lead people to make selfish decisions. Is what makes you feel good always the right thing to do?

DUTY

If you follow this way of thinking it means always doing the right thing by other people even if you suffer as a result. Good behaviour requires you to follow duties. These are things that are self-evidently good, such as helping people in pain, but they do not include things that are just nice to have, such as seeking pleasure or wealth.

WHO CAN TELL?

Can we tell if a choice is right or wrong if we don't know the impact it will have in the future? Should we consider what future humans might want, even though they don't yet exist?

MIND MAP

You've reached the end of the book and now know a lot about the human body and how it might change in the future, but what do you think about it? After learning about different moral codes, do you think it's right? Or is it ultimately wrong? Are some aspects good? I can't tell you the answer, because there isn't one! You have to make your own informed opinion, but now you have the tools to do just that. This mind map is a starting point to build the big picture of the way the human body might change in the future. There's a lot to get your head around, isn't there? Every subject seems to lead to another, and every question answered ends up with more things to ask. I always think that's what makes this stuff so interesting: the way a wide array of subjects all seems to link together. Makes you think, doesn't it? So, now you have the information, what will your opinion be?

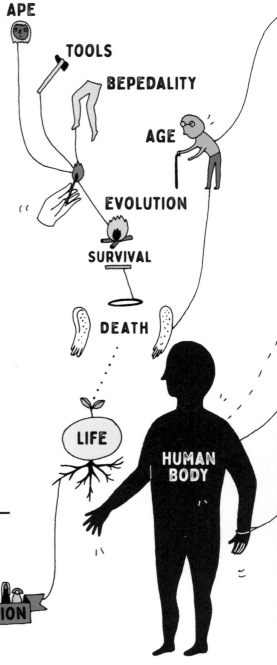

APE

TOOLS

BEPEDALITY

AGE

EVOLUTION

SURVIVAL

DEATH

LIFE

HUMAN BODY

SOCIETY

POPULATION

RACE

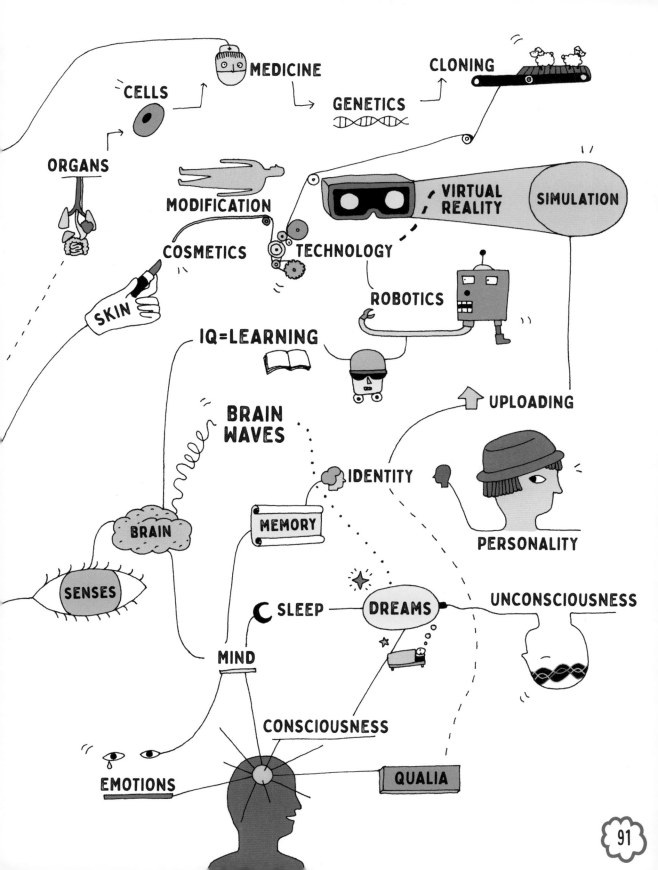

GLOSSARY

antibiotic a medicine that kills bacteria without damaging healthy body parts

ape a primate with no tail – humans are a kind of ape

cell the building block of a living body

consciousness an awareness of the self that humans experience

cybernetic to do with the automatic control of machines

entropy the process by which energy dissipates and matter becomes less ordered

epigenetics where non-genetic features that can change throughout life are inherited from the parents

female the sex that provides the egg cell during fertilisation. The egg cell contains genetic material and the nutrients needed for a new body to begin to grow.

feminine a gender role associated with the female sex but only limited to it by social traditions and conventions

fertility the ability to produce children

fertilisers a chemical that is added to soil to make plants grow faster

free will being able to be in control of your actions

futurology an attempt to predict what will happen in the future based on how technology and society is changing

genetics the study of inheritance, where parents pass genes to their children, which strongly influence how their body will develop

germline the set of cells that produces sex cells (sperm and eggs) which are used in reproduction

infrared an invisible light wave that our skin can detect as heat

IQ standing for intelligence quotient, this is a system for measuring human intelligence that is designed to ignore the influence of education

male the sex that produces sperm cells, which provide genetic material required to make a new body during fertilisation

masculine the gender role associated with the male sex but only limited to it by social traditions and conventions

neuron a nerve cell

nutrients a chemical required by the body to survive and grow; nutrients include sugars, fats, proteins and other essential chemicals called vitamins

oestrus the process of preparing the body for ovulation (egg production), fertilisation and pregnancy

organism a living thing

perception the mental experience created by the brain using inputs from the senses

pigment a coloured chemical

qualia the quality of the experience of colour, sound, taste, etc, which is entirely personal and impossible to compare between people

quantum a small packet of something. In terms of quantum physics, this relates to the way matter and energy are constructed of small packets that cannot be divided up or added to.

tabula rasa meaning 'wiped tablet' or 'clean slate', this term refers to the idea that the human mind and memory is empty of knowledge at birth

ultraviolet an invisible light wave that carries more energy than visible light, which can damage the skin if the energy is not absorbed by dark pigments

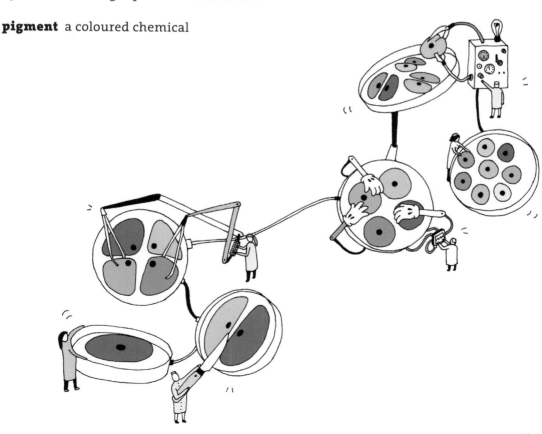

FIND OUT MORE

Now over to you. Use these resources to continue your exploration of all things to do with the human body, the way it works and how it might change in the future. You can find out a lot more in books and on websites. A museum will allow you to study the subject in close-up detail. And these apps and games are a good place to start your career as a futurologist. Good luck!

BOOKS

There aren't many books for young people on futorology, but if you want to read more then try these books for adults.

21 Lessons for the 21st Century, by Yuval Noah Harari, Jonathan Cape, 2018

An Optimist's Tour of the Future, by Mark Stevenson, Profile Books, 2012

The Third Chimpanzee, by Jared Diamond, Triangle Square, 2014

WEBSITES AND ONLINE ARTICLES

The internet is a brilliant resource to answer your niggly questions about futurology. Start with these articles.

BBC Bitesize, Inheritance and Genetics
www.bbc.com/bitesize/topics/zpffr82

Futurology: The Tricky Art of Knowing What Will Happen Next
www.bbc.co.uk/news/magazine-12058575

MUSEUMS

Museums are great places to visit to discover and learn more about the body in an interactive way.

Body Worlds, London, England

Science Museum, London, England

The Hunterian, Glasgow, Scotland

GAMES

You can learn more about how things might change in the future and how society might deal with these changes by playing these games.

Impact: A Foresight Game (board game)

Interactive Brain (online interactive model)
www.brainfacts.org/3D-Brain

Pandemic (board game)

PODCASTS

Listen to people discuss the big questions while on your way to and from school, or at home, with these podcasts.

Flash Forward
A show that discusses possible future scenarios with scientists and experts.

Science Friday
A podcast which discusses scientific concepts in an accessible way.

APPS

Learn more on the go with apps which you can download to your smartphone.

Cyborg Camera, APKPure, (Android)

Cyborg Camera Booth, NOE GUERRERO (iOS)

A FEW FINAL QUESTIONS...

If our current species splits into two or more species in the future – by evolution or by genetic modification – would members of the different species have different rights?

Some suggest that human intelligence will merge with AI computers in the future to become a new form of life. How do you feel about that?

Is there something naturally better about a body that has not been changed or fixed and improved in any way to one that has been? Where do you draw the line – even with medicines or make-up?

INDEX